Does God Matter?

Susan E. Jeans

Fulton, Kentucky

Does God Matter?
Copyright © 2019 by Susan E. Jeans

All rights reserved. No part of this publication may be reproduced, stored in a retrieval system or transmitted in any way by any means, electronic, mechanical, photocopy, recording or otherwise, without the prior permission of the author, except as provided by USA and international copyright law.

Scripture quotations marked AMP are taken from the Amplified Bible, Copyright © 1954, 1958, 1962, 1964, 1965, 1987 by The Lockman Foundation. Used by permission.

Scripture quotations marked BBE are taken from the 1949/1964 BIBLE IN BASIC ENGLISH, public domain.

Scripture quotations marked CEV are from the Contemporary English Version Copyright © 1991, 1992, 1995 by American Bible Society, Used by Permission.

Scripture quotations marked ESV are from The ESV® Bible (The Holy Bible, English Standard Version®), copyright © 2001 by Crossway, a publishing ministry of Good News Publishers. Used by permission. All rights reserved.

Scripture quotations marked KJV are taken from the KING JAMES VERSION (KJV): KING JAMES VERSION, public domain.

Scripture quotations marked NASB are taken from the New American Standard Bible®, Copyright © 1960, 1962, 1963, 1968, 1971, 1972, 1973, 1975, 1977, 1995 by The Lockman Foundation. Used by permission. (www.Lockman.org)

Published by
    Master Design Publishing
    an imprint of Master Design Marketing, LLC
    789 State Route 94 E, Fulton, KY 42041
    www.MasterDesign.org

Cover and interior design by Faithe Thomas.

Print ISBN: 978-1-941512-42-5
Ebook ISBN: 978-1-941512-43-2

Printed in the USA.

*In memory of my beloved sister, Paula,
who learned that God does matter, submitted her life to Jesus,
and has entered into everlasting life with Him.*

Contents

Part One: Why Am I Here on Earth? What Is the Purpose of My Life?........... 1
   Jehovah God.. 3
      There Is a God.. 3
      God's Names.. 3
      Jehovah's Nature 4
   Jehovah's Creation of Two Realms and Rebellions in Both Realms 11
      Heaven, Angels, And the First Rebellion.. 11
      Earth and Man 12
      The Second Rebellion Involving Both Realms 15
      The Third Rebellion Involving Both Realms..................................... 18
   Jehovah's New Nation: From Abraham and His Descendants 25
      The Cost of Sin 28
      Kinsman Redeemer and the Cost of the Redemption of Sin 33
   Why Did Jesus Come? What Is the Message of the Gospel?..................... 35
      Jesus Came as a Man 35
      Jesus Rose from the Dead 37
      Following Jesus.. 38
      Clearing the Land 38
      Summary.. 39
      Only Two Choices in this Life 41
      Jehovah Is Reclaiming the Nations.. 43

Part Two: The Life of a Christian 47
   Living in the Truth 47
   Faith.. 51
   Prayer.. 52
   Spiritual Warfare 55
   Preparing for the Return of Jesus Christ 62

Part Three: In the World But Not of It 75

Afterword 79

Preface

This book started its life as a gift to my grandchildren. At the time of this writing, there are four of them; and they range in age from 4½ years to 18 months. Of course, they are all too young to read, much less to understand what I have written. But they will soon encounter, even at a very tender age, the unfairness and cruelty of life. My desired goal, therefore, was to provide them an overview of the Bible's explanation of why the world is the way it is, and to share with them the Hope that lives within me and gives meaning to my life. I want them to know of this greatest gift that is offered to them as well.

As I wrote, however, my desire to be thorough in my explanations prevailed. The result was a book that is not meant for very young children at all. It is more appropriate for people who are at least in their teens, and probably older. The book for my grandchildren will be my next endeavor!

The purpose of this book remains unchanged from my original intent, and it is my prayer that readers of any age will gain some understanding that they previously lacked. If any reader comes into the family of the Most High God as a result of the reading of this book, then all the glory and thanks goes to "Him who is able to do exceeding abundantly beyond all that we ask or think." Ephesians 3:20

Susan E. Jeans
May 1, 2019

PART ONE

Why am I here on earth? What is the purpose of my life?

Have you ever wondered why you are here on this earth? Is there any purpose or meaning to your life? Every culture that has existed since the dawn of mankind has had its own religion that responds to these questions about the purpose and meaning of life. These man-centered religions range from one extreme of total asceticism (self-denial) to the other extreme of no-holds-barred hedonism (wallowing in indulgence). Even people who claim to be atheists have a religion of their own making; the only difference is that they have not recognized that their "gods" also have names.

The purpose of this book is to give an overview of the answers provided by the only "religion" that is not man-centered, but is rather God-originated and God-centered. Indeed, because God is the Creator of all that exists, both seen and unseen, it is Creator-centered. Christianity is based on the Bible. It is God's Word to us. The New Testament book of 2 Timothy chapter 3, verse 16 says that "all Scripture is breathed out by God." Any so-called Christian denomination that does not rely upon the Bible as its complete authority should not call itself Christian. At the point that man adds to or subtracts from the Bible, that religion has made man, and not God, the ultimate authority, and is thus just one more of many man-centered religions.

In this book, I will summarize the Bible's explanation for why the world is the way it is; what hope there is while we are here in the world; and why God does matter—for now and for eternity. I will also briefly summarize what the future holds for those who have been adopted into the family of God.

Does God Matter?

• 1 •
Jehovah God

THERE IS A GOD

The Bible begins with the premise that there is a God. The major theme or message of the Bible is that He loves you and wants to have a relationship with you. It is not a relationship of tyrant master and subservient slave, but rather a relationship of family, with a loving Father and loving children who desire to please their Father. This God is not visible to you, the way your earthly family members are, so He has revealed Himself to all of us through the Bible. In the Bible, He tells us about Himself, His ways, and His people. For that reason, the Bible is also known as His Word. The Bible is divided into two sections: the Old Testament and the New Testament.

GOD'S NAMES

God has a name. You may think that His name is God, but really that is more like a description. If you are a male, you could be described as a human being, a man, a son, a brother, a nephew, a husband, and a father. But you also have a name. Because the Old Testament was written in Hebrew, the names of God are also in Hebrew. God first gave His name in Exodus 3:14. The closest we can come to saying that name in English is Yahweh (pronounced yaw-way). Another way it is said in English is Jehovah, which can be pronounced as Je-HOE-vah, or as Yay-hoe-VAH. The name means "I AM." What this tells us about Him is that, unlike us, He did not have a beginning; He was not born, as we were. He always existed. It is hard for us to imagine what eternity is, going both backward and forward in time, but He has always existed, He exists now, and He will always exist. He created time and space, so really He existed even before time, and even now, exists outside of time.

Besides Yahweh and Jehovah, He is known by other names in the Bible. The most common is El, which means God. Often it is combined with some other word that describes what He is or what He can do. The names are all Hebrew, but here are some of them:

- El Elyon (God Most High)
- El Roi (God Who Sees)
- El Shaddai (God, the All-Sufficient One; also God Almighty)
- Jehovah Rapha (God Who Heals)
- Jehovah Nissi (The Lord is my Banner)
- Jehovah Shammah (The Lord is There)
- Jehovah Jireh (God Who Provides)
- Jehovah Shalom (The Lord is Peace).

Based on these Hebrew names, He is also called, in English, the Most High, or the Most High God. Now that you know that God has many names, from now on, I will use the name Jehovah when I talk about Him.

JEHOVAH'S NATURE

Jehovah is a spirit being. That means He doesn't have a body, as we do. That also makes it impossible for us to see Him or to reach out to know Him. The only reason we can know Him at all is that He has reached out to us, and made Himself known to us. And He has done that because He loves us and wants us to be a part of His family.

HOLINESS

The primary characteristic of Jehovah that is set out in various ways throughout the Bible is His holiness. It is a word that is associated with Jehovah Himself because only He is holy. This means He is perfect in purity and in moral perfection. He is not only perfectly good, but He is the definition of good. In other words, He defines, He gives meaning to the word, "good." There is no taint of anything less than absolute perfection in His being and in His actions. He cannot be corrupted or brought down or made less than He is. Further, no corrupting influence can be allowed in His presence.

Not only is God Himself holy, but also anything belonging to Him is holy. The word "holy" in Hebrew means to be set apart and to treat as sacred, very special. For example, we may have dishes that we use every day, but then we have a special set of dishes that we use only on special occasions, like Christmas. That special set is "set apart" to be used only at certain times. Everything that was to be used in the worship of Jehovah was also set apart, holy, and could not be used for any other purpose.

Holiness can be a difficult concept to understand. Think of it this way. If there were no evil, bad things in the world, then there would be no need for holiness. That is because holiness is the opposite reaction to evil. Holiness is like the hatred of evil, in any form.

Immutability

Another important characteristic of Jehovah is immutability. This means that He does not change. We can observe how He behaved in certain circumstances as they are recorded in the Bible and know that, under the same circumstances today, He will behave in the same way. We can rely on and trust Him to be consistent.

Omniscience

Jehovah also knows every last little thing about every single thing He ever created. He knows exactly how our bodies work, because He made them, and He knows how our minds work, too. He can hear every thought we think, and every word we say, and He knows, even better than we do, why we do what we do. This ability to know everything, all at once, and always, is called omniscience. No one besides Jehovah has this ability. He is the only Creator, and He knows all about everything He created.

SOVEREIGNTY

Jehovah is sovereign over all His creation. He has the final say and the final control over everyone and everything. No one can thwart His will. Even evil beings can do their harm only within the prescribed limits of His control. He has goals and purposes in the life of each person He created, and He works with their choices and mistakes, their successes and their failures, to help them reach those goals. He allows all created beings, both good and bad, to do as they wish, but He orchestrates circumstances and events, even evil things, to accomplish His will.

Another feature of both His sovereignty and His omniscience is His ability to tell us the end from the beginning. Prophecy, in the sense of foretelling the future, is a major component of the entire Bible. It is one of the ways in which He validates to us that He is the God Most High and there is no other besides Him.

OMNIPRESENCE

Jehovah also has the ability to *be* everywhere in His creation at the same time. Again, He is the only being with this ability. Not one of His created beings can do this. Although He lives in a different dimension or plane, He created this dimension in which we human beings live. He can be in this dimension as well as in the dimension of the spirit at the same time. In the Bible, there are times when Jehovah says something like this: "I will go down and see if what I hear is true." But He already knows the answer, because He knows everything all the time, and He is already present everywhere at the same time. This is just one way that the Bible says something so that we will understand. It is called anthropomorphism. It means that we use expressions as if Jehovah were a human man instead of a spirit, because it makes it easier for us to understand what He is doing. So when the Bible uses expressions like "the hand of God," we have to remember that He is a spirit, so He would not have hands like yours and mine.

Omnipotence

Jehovah is the most powerful being that exists now or has ever existed or ever will exist. This characteristic is called omnipotence. Some of His created beings are also very powerful, but no one, absolutely no one—human or spirit—is more powerful than Jehovah. There is no equality between Jehovah and any of His created beings. You may read, perhaps in prayer books, that Jehovah is described as Almighty God. The word "Almighty" is another word that depicts His omnipotence.

Jehovah is also the only being Who can create something out of nothing. We can create things, too, like knitting a blanket, or painting a picture, or writing a story, but we can't create the things that made our creations possible. Using the example of knitting a blanket, we can't create the sheep to grow the wool for the yarn for the blanket, and we can't create the bamboo tree from which the knitting needles are made.

Just/Merciful

Jehovah is also perfectly just. He will always act in accordance with what is morally right. His decisions are always well-founded in His laws and precepts, and each person will receive exactly the treatment he or she deserves, no more and no less. It is impossible for Him to be prejudiced or partisan. He is always impartial. Because He is perfectly righteous, there are no surprises in His judgments. This legal aspect of His character is demonstrated frequently in the Old Testament, as, for example, when He calls upon heaven and earth to witness His faithfulness to His people, and their unfaithfulness to Him. His adherence to His own laws is demonstrated in the New Testament most graphically with the crucifixion of Jesus Christ. He cannot show mercy until justice has been met. When the sins of the world were paid for by Jesus Christ, then His justice was fully satisfied, and He was free to show mercy.

In this world, you see examples of injustice everywhere. On a test at school, one student cheats, but is not caught, so he gets a higher score than you did, even though you studied hard and did your very best. Or you and a friend are both driving your cars over the speed limit, but only you get caught and ticketed, and your friend speeds off, laughing because he was not caught. Or your boss favors one of your co-workers over the others, and lets him get away with not doing his job, but if you fail to do the same job, you get marked down on your performance evaluation. For the time being, evil rules this world that we live in. We will talk about this in the very next section when we learn about rebellions. For now, it is important to know that Jehovah sees and knows exactly what is going on in every single person's life, and He will make things right, if not while we are alive on earth, then after that. It is not our job to get even with someone who hurts us. That is Jehovah's job and He will be sure to do it.

While Jehovah will make sure that every single person who has ever lived, or who ever will live, will come before Him and will be rewarded or punished for his behavior on earth, He loves us so much that He has provided a way to be merciful to us. Even when we deserve to be punished, He will instead, under certain circumstances, give us mercy. He will not punish us as we deserve.

This love of His is so great that we can't even begin to grasp it in our minds and hearts. He shows us this love in one huge, mind-blowing move. Because He is just, Jehovah cannot allow bad things to go unpunished. Think how you felt when you got punished for doing something wrong, but your friend, who was doing the same thing, was not. All bad things must, and will be punished. If Jehovah did not punish all bad things, then He would not be just. But He loves you so much that He sent His Son, Jesus, to become a human man, and made Him take all the punishment that everyone deserves for all the bad things they have done. Jesus was punished in the place of all people, and in your place, too, because you have done bad things as well. And, for all those who accept that Jesus took their punishment and who want to be like Jesus and love Jehovah back, they will escape the punishment that they already deserve, no matter how young or how old they are! That's a lot of love, isn't it?

The Trinity

There is another aspect of God's nature that is so difficult to understand that I don't believe there is one person on earth who really grasps it fully. We just have to accept that this is so because the Bible sets it out. I am talking about the Trinity. God exists in three distinct Persons, and yet they are all still one God. When the Bible is referring to the Trinity, it uses the Hebrew name Elohim (pronounced el-o-HEEM). It is telling us that there is one God, but He exists in three Persons. The first is Jehovah, also called God the Father. The second is Jesus Christ, also called God the Son. And the third is called God the Holy Spirit. Of these, only Jesus Christ, God the Son, left the heavenly realm to become a human being, just like us. He was the physical expression of His Father, the perfect image of Jehovah. Thus, if one came to know Jesus, that person would also know Jehovah. Jesus lived as a human being about 2,000 years ago, so we can't meet Him in person today, but we can still know Him through the words that He spoke, which are in the Bible, and through God the Holy Spirit. We will talk more about God the Holy Spirit later.

We speak of all the members of the Trinity as male, rather than female. We say God the Father, God the Son, and God the Holy Spirit. And we use the masculine pronouns, "He," "Him," and "His." We do this for two reasons. The first is that it is what Jesus (God the Son) did when He was a man on earth. And He, being God Himself, ought to know! The second is that we learn from the Bible that God (Elohim, the Trinity) rules over all creation the same way. That means that the same order of authority was established everywhere. And in the two realms that He created, the male was given headship. Don't misunderstand me and think that girls and women are not as important as boys and men. The Bible makes it abundantly clear that they are all of equal value to Jehovah. They simply have different roles and job assignments.

DOES GOD MATTER?

• 2 •
Jehovah's Creation of Two Realms and Rebellions in Both Realms

HEAVEN, ANGELS, AND THE FIRST REBELLION

Before Jehovah created earth and put people on it to live here, He had already created a different realm, one that is invisible to us. We usually call that realm "heaven" but it can also be known as the "celestial realm." Like Jehovah, the inhabitants of the celestial realm are spirit beings. They don't have bodies as we do. In the Bible, these spirit beings have different names and job descriptions, like angels, stars, cherubim, seraphim, living creatures, sons of God, and even "gods." In Hebrew, the word for "gods" is the same as one of the Hebrew names for God. That word is elohim. *That* is why it is important to know God's proper name, like Jehovah or Jesus, so that, when you call upon Him, everyone in the celestial realm knows you are not calling upon one of the other beings.

Jehovah filled this celestial realm with these various creatures whom He loved and whom He allowed to help Him in the day-to-day operations of heaven. (By the way, this realm is invisible only to us; the spirit beings who live there can see each other!) They were created to represent Him and His will in the carrying out of their assigned responsibilities. Perhaps we could compare it to a family business, and Jehovah included all the family members in the running of His operations.

When you were a child, playing with a transformer or a stuffed animal or a doll, you made it do whatever you wanted it to do. You moved it, you talked for it, you played with it. But when Jehovah created the spirit beings who would live in His celestial realm (let's call them all "angels" for now), He did not want a toy angel that would do and say whatever He wanted. He loved His angels and He wanted the angels He created to freely love Him back. And the only way that they could freely love Him back was to give them the freedom to choose not to love Him back. This freedom to love or not to love is called free will. The angels could freely choose to love or not to love Jehovah, their Creator. And, while Jehovah is perfect and will always do what is right, His created angels were and are not perfect, and therefore they were and are capable of choosing what is wrong. Some did love Him back and happily served in their assigned jobs, but some did not. Some did not want to serve the One Who had created them. They did not want to help run the operations of the family business. And at least one, called Satan, wanted to take the place of Jehovah Himself! The result was that there were and still are both good angels and rebellious, bad angels in heaven. The rebellious spirits are often called fallen angels.

EARTH AND MAN

At some unknown point after the rebellion of some of the angels (remember, we are just using the word "angels" to describe all the spirit beings other than Jehovah/the Trinity in the celestial realm), Jehovah decided, for His own reasons, that He wanted to have a human family as well as a heavenly family. It's not that He needs anything or anyone. He doesn't. He is complete in Himself. But the Bible tells us that He is love, and He wanted to create people to love and enjoy and for our love and enjoyment as well. So He created the earth, and made it perfect for human habitation, and then He created a man and a woman to live on the earth. The Bible calls them Adam and Eve. They were assigned two jobs. The first was that they were to have lots of children so that there would be more people on the earth. And the second was that they were supposed to govern the earth as Jehovah's assistants. Just as His heavenly assistants helped in the day-to-day operations of heaven and were a part of His heavenly family, Jehovah intended that Adam and Eve would be His earthly assistants and be part of His earthly family. The Bible says that people were created in the image of God. We were meant to serve as His representatives on earth. He wanted His creation, the people, to help in the operation of His earth.

Just as the Trinitarian God exists in three Persons, He created people in three parts. One is the physical body, which we can see and touch. Another is the soul. This cannot be seen with our eyes, but it is what makes each individual one-of-a-kind. It is what makes you you. It is where you think, make decisions, and have feelings like anger or happiness. The third part is the spirit. This is the part of us through which we can sense spiritual things. It is the spirit part of Adam and Eve that communicated with Jehovah when they lived in His presence on the earth. Just as two of the three Persons of the Trinity cannot be seen, two of the three parts that make up a person cannot be seen.

In the same manner as He had with His created angels, Jehovah gave Adam and Eve the same free will to love Him back and to help Him govern the earth. He asked them to obey His command not to eat the fruit of one particular tree, warning them that, if they did, they would die on that day. But Satan took on the physical form of a serpent, and came to Eve, and convinced her that Jehovah did not really love her because He was not giving her all she deserved to have! He told her that Jehovah did not want her to eat the fruit of that particular tree because, if she did, she would become like Jehovah Himself. The serpent tricked Eve into believing lies about Jehovah—that He was not good and would not take care of her. And she also believed the lie that she could become like a god herself. Although the Bible does not tell us where Adam was while the serpent and Eve were having this conversation, it does state explicitly in 1 Timothy 2:14 that Adam was not deceived. Nevertheless, he must have also believed the serpent's lie that he could become like a god himself, because when Eve offered Adam the forbidden fruit, he also ate it. This event is called the Fall of Mankind.

Remember that Jehovah had warned Adam and Eve that they would die on the day that they ate the fruit of the one tree forbidden to them. And they did, though not in the way that the serpent had undoubtedly hoped. Death means separation, and on that day, Jehovah expelled Adam and Eve from His presence. They could no longer live with Him. In addition, the spirit part of them, the part that allowed them to sense spiritual things, died. Their rebellion had cost them everlasting life with their Creator. Their rebellion also resulted in a change in their nature. It became a rebellious nature, a sin nature. It is a nature that automatically wants the opposite of what Jehovah wants for us. From that time on, all human beings were and are born with this sin nature. It is now natural for people to rebel against authority. Children are born selfish and self-centered, and they rebel against their parents, because they want what *they* want, and do not understand that their parents have rules for the good of the children. Adults rebel against the rules and laws of society because they are also self-centered and selfish and want to set their own rules. Like Adam and Eve, people of all ages still believe the lie of the serpent that they can be like gods themselves.

Another thing happened when Adam and Eve were separated from Jehovah. Remember that Jehovah had told them to govern the earth as His assistants. At the Fall, Adam and Eve lost the right to serve as His assistants, and the evil fallen angels, led by Satan, also called the devil, took over the rulership of the world. And all human beings born after the Fall not only have this sin nature, but are actually born under the authority of Satan. In a very real way, they are children of Satan (though they are slaves of Satan as well), even though they are still made in the image of Jehovah. They have the same rebellious nature as Satan, and naturally behave as he does.

Whether we like it or not, Jehovah created us to be under authority. He meant for us to be under *His* authority, because that is when we will be happy and fulfilled. But because of the Fall of Adam and Eve, we are born with rebellious natures and are under the authority, whether we admit it or not, and whether we like it or not, of Satan (the devil, the accuser, the evil one, a liar and the father of lies, and the deceiver, among other things).

THE SECOND REBELLION INVOLVING BOTH REALMS

This second rebellion is described in vague terms in Genesis 6:1-4. When I quote from the Bible, I will often give two English translations. The first is a very exact translation from Hebrew to English (if the quote is from the Old Testament) or from Greek to English (if the quote is from the New Testament). The second is not an exact translation, but it tells us what happened in the way that people talk today.

> Genesis 6:1-4 ESV (English Standard Version)
> *¹When man began to multiply on the face of the land and daughters were born to them, ²the **sons of God** saw that the daughters of man were attractive. And they took as their wives any they chose. ³Then the Lord said, "My Spirit shall not abide in man forever, for he is flesh: his days shall be 120 years." ⁴The Nephilim were on the earth in those days, and also afterward, when the sons of God came in to the daughters of man and they bore children to them. These were the mighty men who were of old, the men of renown.*

> Genesis 6:1-4 CEV (Contemporary English Version)
> ¹More and more people were born, until finally they spread all over the earth. ²Some of their daughters were so beautiful that **supernatural beings** came down and married the ones they wanted. ³Then the Lord said, "I won't let my life-giving breath remain in anyone forever. No one will live for more than one hundred twenty years." ⁴The children of the supernatural beings who had married these women became famous heroes and warriors. They were called Nephilim and lived on the earth at that time and even later.

Scholars who write about the Bible disagree about the identity of the "sons of God" in this ESV translation. "Sons of God" is a literal translation of the Hebrew. As the CEV version interprets it, they were supernatural beings who came down to earth from the celestial realm. My opinion agrees with both the ESV and the CEV. These so-called "sons of God" were from the celestial or heavenly realm. That's why the CEV describes them as "supernatural beings." Unless they were on an assignment to earth from Jehovah, these supernatural beings, sons of God, whom we are calling "angels," were supposed to stay in the heavenly realm. In violation of this, some of them came to earth, took on the physical form of men, and had babies with human women. The children were half human and half "angel." They were called Nephilim. Elsewhere in the Bible they are called giants and Anakim and Rephaim. Jehovah was very angry, because these fallen angels and their children made human people even more sinful and wicked and evil than they already were because of the sinful nature they inherited from Adam after the Fall. The next verses of Genesis tell us that He was upset that His intention to have a spirit family in heaven and a human family on earth had been spoiled by the bad spirit beings, which we are calling fallen angels. What was now on earth was a new species of hybrid human/angel beings that were giant-sized and powerful — and, although it does not tell us in this passage, destructive. Jehovah decided to send a flood upon the earth to destroy all people, which would include the hybrid Nephilim giants, and animals and birds.

Genesis 6:5-7 ESV

5 The Lord saw that the wickedness of man was great in the earth, and that every intention of the thoughts of his heart was only evil continually. 6And the Lord was sorry that He had made man on the earth, and it grieved Him to His heart. 7So the Lord said, "I will blot out man whom I have created from the face of the land, man and animals and creeping things and birds of the heavens, for I am sorry that I have made them."

> Genesis 6:5-7 CEV
>
> *⁵The Lord saw how bad the people on earth were and that everything they thought and planned was evil. ⁶He was very sorry that He had made them, ⁷and He said, "I'll destroy every living creature on earth! I'll wipe out people, animals, birds, and reptiles. I'm sorry I ever made them."*

Jehovah can see into our hearts and minds (after all, He created us), so He knows us better than we know ourselves. He could see that there was one man who had his heart set on obeying Jehovah. So Jehovah told that man, Noah, to build a large boat, called an ark, before He sent the flood. In this ark, Jehovah would save Noah and his family, and two of some kinds of animals and birds, and seven of other kinds. It took a long time to build such a boat. Bible scholars think that the reference to 120 years in Genesis 6:3 means it took Noah that long to build an ark large enough to hold his family and all those animals, and that during that time, Noah was warning other people about the coming flood, but they didn't pay any attention to him. I think it is reasonable to assume that many people made fun of Noah and laughed at him.

At the appointed time, the flood came. Because Noah and his family were the only people saved, the flood is often referred to as the Noahic flood, and the events of human history that happened before this flood are known as ante-diluvian.

When the flood waters subsided, so that the ark was no longer floating on water, but rather was sitting on land, Noah and his family and all the animals left the ark. Once more, as He had done with Adam and Eve, Jehovah commanded Noah and his family to have lots of children and to spread over all the earth and fill it. He also allowed people to eat the meat of animals and fish. Before the flood, people ate only plants. Jehovah also promised that He would never again destroy all living things by a world-wide flood, and He gave the rainbow in the sky as a sign of His promise. Whenever a rainbow appears in the sky, people can remember His promise.

THE THIRD REBELLION INVOLVING BOTH REALMS

Despite Jehovah's command to spread out over all the earth and to fill it, people decided not to obey it. As they all spoke the same language, they decided to build a city and stay together. As we have seen from other quotations from the Bible, Jehovah is called the Lord.

Genesis 11:4-9 ESV

⁴Then they said, "Come, let us build ourselves a city and a tower with its top in the heavens, and let us make a name for ourselves, **lest we be dispersed over the face of the whole earth."** *⁵And the Lord came down to see the city and the tower, which the children of man had built. ⁶And the Lord said, "Behold, they are one people, and they have all one language, and this is only the beginning of what they will do. And nothing that they propose to do will now be impossible for them. ⁷Come, let us go down and there confuse their language, so that they may not understand one another's speech."* **⁸So the Lord dispersed them from there over the face of all the earth,** *and they left off building the city. ⁹Therefore its name was called Babel, because there the Lord confused the language of all the earth. And from there the Lord dispersed them over the face of all the earth.*

Genesis 11:1-8 CEV

¹At first everyone spoke the same language, ²but after some of them moved from the east and settled in Babylonia, ³⁻⁴they said: "Let's build a city with a tower that reaches to the sky! We'll use hard bricks and tar instead of stone and mortar. We'll become famous, and **we won't be scattered all over the world**." ⁵But when the Lord came down to look at the city and the tower, ⁶He said: "These people are working together because they all speak the same language. This is just the beginning. Soon they will be able to do anything they want. ⁷Come on! Let's go down and

confuse them by making them speak different languages-then they won't be able to understand each other." ⁸⁻⁹ So the people had to stop building the city, because **the Lord confused their language and scattered them all over the earth**. *That's how the city of Babel got its name.*

In the next chapter of Genesis, chapter 12, Jehovah picked out Abraham (who was called Abram until Jehovah changed his name) and told him that He would bless him and make a new nation from this man's descendants. Abraham and his wife had wanted children but had been unable to have them. But at a time when they were considered too old to be able to have children, Jehovah made it possible, and they had a son named Isaac. When Isaac was grown, he got married and he and his wife had twin sons, Esau and Jacob. Jacob married and had 12 sons and at least one daughter. Jehovah gave Jacob a new name, Israel, and his 12 sons became the 12 tribes of Israel. Their descendants are now, approximately 4,000 years later, the nation of Israel.

It is not until later in the Bible, in the book of Deuteronomy, that we learn what happened to the rest of the people in the world after Jehovah scattered them at Babel. And this is where the celestial, or heavenly realm, comes into the picture again. Just before the 12 tribes of Israel were to re-enter the land of Israel, Moses (a leader of the people of Israel) gave a speech, in which he referred to Jehovah as the Most High:

> Deuteronomy 32:7-9 ESV
>
> *⁷Remember the days of old; consider the years of many generations; ask your father, and he will show you, your elders, and they will tell you. ⁸When the Most High gave to the nations their inheritance, when He divided mankind, He fixed the borders of the peoples according to the number of the sons of God. ⁹But the Lord's portion is His people, Jacob His allotted heritage.*

> Deuteronomy 32:7-10 CEV
> *⁷Think about past generations. Ask your parents or any of your elders. They will tell you ⁸that God Most High gave land to every nation. He assigned a guardian angel to each of them, ⁹but the Lord Himself takes care of Israel.*

What these verses are telling us is that, after Jehovah scattered the people at Babel, He divided the land and the people into nations, according to the number of "the sons of God" (ESV). The CEV (Contemporary English Version) correctly explains that the sons of God are the members of the heavenly or celestial family, by calling them "guardian angels." These heavenly beings were each assigned to watch over and oversee the human governance of a particular land and nation. While all of Jehovah's creation belongs to Him, He would deal with the nations only indirectly, handing over the charge of them to His angels, the "sons of God." Only Israel, the new nation which Jehovah was creating from Abraham, would belong directly to the Lord, and would be overseen and guarded by Jehovah Himself.

So far, in this third rebellion against Jehovah, we have seen that on earth, people didn't want to obey Him. They wanted to focus on making themselves great, and the result was that Jehovah scattered them and gave them different languages, and, most importantly, gave them over to be watched by His angels, instead of directly by Himself. (Remember, we are calling all the beings, other than Jehovah, in the heavenly realm "angels," although there are many different kinds of beings, with different names and job assignments.) Then the third rebellion happened in the heavenly realm. The Bible does not tell us when this happened or how long it took, but the angels apparently let the power go to their heads. Instead of influencing the people to look to Jehovah and to worship Him, they influenced the people to worship them (the angels) as gods. These angels became corrupt and fallen. And many of the lesser angels who worked for them also fell.

There is an account of the effect of this fall in the Old Testament book of Daniel, chapter 10, verses 12-21. Daniel had been given a vision which had troubled him, and he had prayed for understanding. Jehovah had heard Daniel's prayer and had immediately sent an angel to go in visible form to Daniel and give an explanation. But the angel was held up by a bad or fallen angel, who was called the prince of the kingdom of Persia. This powerful fallen angel fought against him to keep him from reaching Daniel. Finally, after 21 days, a very powerful good angel, named Michael, came to help him and he made it to Daniel. The fallen angel is called the prince of Persia, because he was the once-good angel who had been assigned to guard over the nation where Daniel was, which was at that time called Persia. Today that nation is called Iran.

The key verse in Daniel chapter 10 is verse 13:

Daniel 10:13 ESV
The prince of the kingdom of Persia withstood me twenty-one days, but Michael, one of the chief princes, came to help me, for I was left there with the kings of Persia.

Daniel 10:13 CEV
But the guardian angel of Persia opposed me for twenty-one days. Then Michael, who is one of the strongest guardian angels, came to rescue me from the kings of Persia.

Jehovah will at some time in the future judge these once-good angels (the "sons of God") who became corrupt and bad. This is set out in Psalms chapter 82. Let me explain some terms in the verses which follow. The divine council is a description of a group of celestial beings that includes once-good angels who were assigned to watch over all the nations except Israel. They are the "gods" of verse 1 whom God/Jehovah is judging. In verses 2-4, Jehovah is talking to those angels, criticizing them in verse 2 for their bad behavior. In verses 3 and 4, He explains what they should have been doing. Verse 5 describes the fallen nature of these angels who were supposed to guard and watch over all the nations other than Israel. They didn't care or try to understand what they were supposed to be doing. Verses 6 and 7 describe the judgment that Jehovah is pronouncing over these bad angels. They were once sons of the Most High, His sons, and they were described as gods, but, at some time in the future, they will die. As celestial beings, they are spirit in form and have immortality. Since death means separation, their death will be their complete separation from Jehovah's presence. They will spend eternity in the lake of fire that was "prepared for the devil and his angels" (Matthew 25:41). In the last verse of Psalms chapter 82, the writer speaks to Jehovah, and asks Him for His just judgment, because all the nations belong to Him.

Psalms 82 ESV

¹God has taken His place in the divine council; in the midst of the gods He holds judgment: ²"How long will you judge unjustly and show partiality to the wicked? ³Give justice to the weak and the fatherless; maintain the right of the afflicted and the destitute. ⁴Rescue the weak and the needy; deliver them from the hand of the wicked." ⁵ They have neither knowledge nor understanding, they walk about in darkness; all the foundations of the earth are shaken. ⁶I said, "You are gods, sons of the Most High, all of you; ⁷nevertheless, like men you shall die, and fall like any prince." ⁸Arise, O God, judge the earth; for you shall inherit all the nations!

Psalms 82 CEV

¹When all of the other gods have come together, the Lord God judges them and says: ²"How long will you keep judging unfairly and favoring evil people? ³Be fair to the poor and to orphans. Defend the helpless and everyone in need. ⁴Rescue the weak and homeless from the powerful hands of heartless people. ⁵None of you know or understand a thing. You live in darkness, while the foundations of the earth tremble. ⁶I, the Most High God, say that all of you are gods and also my own children. ⁷But you will die, just like everyone else, including powerful rulers." ⁸Do something, God! Judge the nations of the earth; they belong to you.

What we can know so far is that there are good and bad angels in the heavenly realm, just as there are good and bad people on earth. But the two realms are connected. **What happens in the heavenly realm affects what happens on earth and what happens on earth also affects the heavenly realm.**

• 3 •
Jehovah's New Nation: From Abraham And His Descendants

As we saw in the last section, Jehovah decided to create a new nation, Israel. He would begin again to make an earthly family, starting with Abraham. Because our own entry into the human side of Jehovah's family ties into Abraham, it is important to understand now *how* Abraham was chosen to be the first of the earthly family of God. It is not because Abraham was better than other men, or because he was good at following rules, or because he never did anything that displeased Jehovah, or because he did many things that did please Jehovah. Jehovah reached out to Abraham first, and gave Abraham promises. All Abraham did was believe that Jehovah would keep His promises. That is called faith. Faith means that we believe that what Jehovah says is true. It means that we believe that He will keep His promises. He says what He means, and He means what He says.

Like Abraham, we can never *be* good enough. We can never keep rules perfectly. We have done and will do many things that will displease Him. We will never be able to do enough to *earn* our way into His family. Like Abraham, all we have to do is believe what He says. We must believe that He keeps His promises, both for reward and for punishment. Like Abraham, we must have faith.

To this new nation of Israel, made up of the 12 tribes descended from Abraham, Isaac, and Jacob, this nation that He Himself had called into existence, Jehovah began anew to reveal Himself. The entire history of the nation of Israel, as it is recorded in the Old Testament, is the revelation of Jehovah's holiness, His perfection, His love, His justice, His unchangeableness, His patience, and His love.

Just as we have seen that Jehovah has many names in the Bible, there are several different names for this nation of people descended from Abraham. Approximately 1,400 years after Jehovah called Abraham, the people of Israel went into captivity in Babylon for 70 years. Up to that time, the descendants of Abraham had been called the Hebrews or the Israelites. At the time of the Babylonian captivity, they began to be called Jews. And that is what the people who are descended from Abraham are called today: Jews. Those who live today in the nation of Israel are called Israelis. Because Israel allows non-Jews to become Israeli citizens, not all Israelis are Jews.

When He first created human beings, Jehovah had made it plain that there were some rules that applied to all human life. For example, people were forbidden to kill one another, and if they did, then the murderer must himself be killed. But later in Israel's history, Jehovah provided Israel with a complex set of laws, called the Law of Moses, or the Mosaic Law, governing every aspect of their lives, from what foods they could eat and how they were to prepare those foods, to how they were to approach Him in the tabernacle that they had built according to His detailed instructions. With the advanced scientific knowledge that we have today, we know now that the rules about food preparation prevented food poisoning, and kept the people healthier. Another rule, about letting the land rest every seventh year, kept the soil from becoming too depleted. Many of the health rules prevented or at least slowed the spread of infection. If the people kept all the rules governing their daily lives, they would be healthier than all the surrounding nations. Those nations might then wonder what it was that Israel had that made them so well, and they might be drawn to Israel's God, Jehovah. In fact, Jehovah told Israel that He intended them to be a nation of priests. Priests are people who stand between man and Jehovah and represent Jehovah before the people and also represent the people before Jehovah. Jehovah wanted Israel to be His representative to the other nations of the world, so that they would then be drawn to Him.

As a nation, the Jews were privileged above all the other nations of the earth. Jehovah had created this nation for Himself. The Jews were His "chosen people." It was to them that Jehovah gave the special rules, the Mosaic Law. Had the people kept these rules, and lived by them, He would have made them the most blessed of all nations. Unfortunately, the Jews were also infected with the sin nature, the rebellious nature that all people have had since Adam. They began to feel that they were better than any of the people of the other nations, people whom they called Gentiles. When they used that word, Gentiles, they meant it as an insult. In addition, they lost their respect for Jehovah, and began to get lazy about following His rules. Their feelings about Jehovah went from bad to worse, from disrespect and laziness to outright rejection of Him. They began to worship the gods of the other nations. And we already know that the "gods" that the other nations worshiped were the fallen angels whom Jehovah had put in charge of those other nations.

Occasionally, there would be a man who, although he also had a sin nature, would have a heart that was respectful of Jehovah. Some of these men were called prophets, because Jehovah would speak to them, and they would repeat to the people what He had told them. The words that Jehovah gave were mostly warnings to stop worshiping the false gods of the other nations, but He also reminded them constantly of His love for them, and He asked the people again and again to return to Him. No matter what they did to Him, He was always faithful to keep His word. That included blessings when they obeyed Him, and punishment when they did not. He was very patient with them, giving them hundreds of years to return to Him. Finally, He split the nation of Israel into two parts, and allowed both parts to be conquered by other nations that treated them cruelly, and killed many of them.

Before we go any further in this story of the Bible, there are two other concrete pictures from the Old Testament that demonstrate how far Jehovah was willing to go in order to have His desired loving human family on earth. The first is the cost of sin. And the second is the concept of the kinsman redeemer.

THE COST OF SIN

Even before the Mosaic Law was given, Genesis 3:21 tells us:
And the Lord God made for Adam and for his wife garments of skins and clothed them. ESV

Then the Lord God made clothes out of animal skins for the man and his wife. CEV

In order to make clothing of animal skins, Jehovah (the Lord God) had to kill some animals. At the very beginning, at the very first sin, something in the creation had to die to cover the sin. When an animal or a person is killed, their blood is spilled out. So spilled blood came to represent a life that had been killed.

After the flood, when Jehovah allowed Noah to eat animals as well as plants, He told them:

Genesis 9:4 ESV
But you shall not eat flesh with its life, that is, its blood.

Genesis 9:4 CEV
But life is in the blood, and you must not eat any meat that still has blood in it.

Later, the blood of an animal was used as a sign of protection. Before Moses was given the Law (the set of rules) for the people of Israel, Moses was instructed by Jehovah to tell the people of Israel to kill a lamb and to put its blood on the two doorposts and the lintel over the door of their houses. Through Moses, Jehovah said to the people:

Exodus 12:13 ESV
The blood shall be a sign for you, on the houses where you are. And when I see the blood, I will pass over you, and no plague will befall you to destroy you, when I strike the land of Egypt.

> Exodus 12:13 CEV
> *The blood on the houses will show me where you live, and when I see the blood, I will pass over you. Then you won't be bothered by the terrible disasters I will bring on Egypt.*

When Moses was given the Law, a large part of the rules governed the process of sacrificing (killing) animals as a way of covering their sins so that they could come to worship Jehovah. It was a very detailed set of rules. One major point that the people were meant to see from this was that their sins were very serious to Jehovah, so much so that, even though they sinned unintentionally, an animal had to be killed to pay for it. The animals had to be sacrificed, which means their blood had to be spilled. The priests who killed the animals would be covered in the blood of the animals.

By the way, all this was just for unintentional sins. That means something you did wrong, but you didn't mean to do it, or maybe didn't even know at the time that you were doing wrong. If you did something wrong on purpose, there was no animal's death that could cover it. Depending on what the sin was, there was only punishment for the person who sinned, up to and including that person's death.

There were also animal sacrifices for other purposes, such as to give thanks to Jehovah, or to ask for some blessing.

Some of the meat of some of the animal sacrifices could be eaten. But there was one strict rule for all meat:

> Leviticus 7:26-27 ESV
> *[26]Moreover, you shall eat no blood whatever, whether of fowl or of animal, in any of your dwelling places. [27]Whoever eats any blood, that person shall be cut off from his people.*

> Leviticus 7:26-27 CEV
>
> ²⁶*And no matter where you live, you must not eat the blood of any bird or animal, ²⁷or you will no longer belong to the community of Israel.*

This absolute rule against eating the blood of an animal was repeated later, and this time the explanation was given: the life of an animal (or a person) is in the blood. Jehovah was allowing the people to use the blood, which represented the life, of an animal, to pay for the people's sins in the place of the people. Instead of the people being killed and having their own blood to pay for their own sins, the blood of an animal was allowed.

> Leviticus 17:10-14 ESV
>
> *¹⁰If any one of the house of Israel or of the strangers who sojourn among them eats any blood, I will set my face against that person who eats blood and will cut him off from among his people. ¹¹For **the life of the flesh is in the blood**, and I have given it for you on the altar to **make atonement for your souls, for it is the blood that makes atonement by the life**. ¹²Therefore I have said to the people of Israel, No person among you shall eat blood, neither shall any stranger who sojourns among you eat blood. ¹³Any one also of the people of Israel, or of the strangers who sojourn among them, who takes in hunting any beast or bird that may be eaten shall pour out its blood and cover it with earth. ¹⁴For **the life of every creature is its blood: its blood is its life**. Therefore I have said to the people of Israel, You shall not eat the blood of any creature, **for the life of every creature is its blood**. Whoever eats it shall be cut off.*

Even though the people who sinned deserved to die, Jehovah was allowing the people to kill an animal *in their place*. The animal had not sinned, but it was killed in the place of the person who had sinned. The everyday English translation makes this plain:

> Leviticus 17:10-14 CEV
> ¹⁰*I will turn against any of my people who eat blood. This also includes any foreigners living among you.* ¹¹**Life is in the blood, and I have given you the blood of animals to sacrifice in place of your own**. ¹²*That's also why I have forbidden you to eat blood.* ¹³*Even if you should hunt and kill a bird or an animal, you must drain out the blood and cover it with soil.* ¹⁴**The life of every living creature is in its blood.** *That's why I have forbidden you to eat blood and why I have warned you that anyone who does will no longer belong to my people.*

Remember when we were talking about the holiness of Jehovah, in the earlier section about His nature? His goodness and perfection will not allow any badness or imperfection or corruption in His presence. And to be separated from the presence of Jehovah is death. From the minute that we first did one thing wrong, even if we didn't know it was wrong, we deserved to be separated from Jehovah forever. That's how extremely opposite goodness and perfection are from badness and imperfection. And yet, Jehovah had a plan to overcome this problem. He began to show it to people in this system of killing animals who had not done anything wrong *in the place of* the people who had. He was showing people a picture of what He planned to do that would do more than just cover our sins. What He would do would take people's sins away forever!

Other rules in the Mosaic Law dealt with the manner in which people could approach Jehovah. The rules were detailed and extremely specific and there was no leniency, no wiggle-room. The rules were obeyed or the rule-breaker died. The reason it was all so strict is that Jehovah was trying to show to people that He is perfect and holy. Holiness is the reaction of a purely good and perfect God to the existence and presence of evil.

As the Creator of human beings, Jehovah gets to decide who will approach Him and how. After the Fall, all human beings are infected with a sin nature, a rebellious nature. We also have all done bad things. We have sinned against Him. Sin corrupts us, and God, Who is holy, cannot permit sin's corrupting influence in the presence of His absolute perfection. But because He loves us so much, He had decided to provide a way for us to be around Him in a way that He could not only endure, but would actually enjoy. Remember that He very much wants to have a human family to love and to love Him back and to help Him govern the earth.

So, when you read the Old Testament lists of rules and rules and rules about how the priests had to do this and that and the next thing before they could come into the tabernacle that He had them build for their worship of Him, remember that it was all meant to show people that we are not fit to be in His presence, and that we must be made clean by having our sins removed. It was all a picture of the plan He already had made to send His Son, Jesus, into the world, to take our punishment for us.

But rules are important for another reason. It is natural for all people not to like rules, because we are all born with this rebellious nature. You will discover that some people think that Christianity is all about "thou shalt not this" and "thou shalt not that," and there is no fun allowed. Let me give you an example that shows us another reason that rules are important. A man whose son played soccer took his son to a game, but when they got there, the other parents told him that the man who would referee the game would be late. They asked this father to be the referee until the other man arrived. Although the father did not know the rules of the game, he agreed. The result was that fouls were not called when they should have been called, children got hurt, and the parents got really upset. The chaos of the game disappeared when the referee arrived and restored order. The children played according to the rules, fouls were called when it was appropriate, and no one else suffered an injury. When the children played within the confines of the rules, everyone had fun (except perhaps the losing team!).

These examples remind us that Jehovah does not impose rules on us just to be mean or arbitrary. They are for our good. He loves us so much that He wants us to live without hurting ourselves, and we have the best chance of avoiding injury to ourselves and others when we observe those rules.

It is also most important to remember that the rules are not a way to earn your way into becoming a member of Jehovah's family. They are a way of showing Him that you love Him and *want* to be in His family. Obeying His rules is your way of showing your loyalty to Him.

Now let's look at another Old Testament picture that gives us another clue about Jehovah's marvelous, phenomenal, wondrous, amazing plan.

KINSMAN REDEEMER AND THE COST OF THE REDEMPTION OF SIN

The Biblical concept of kinsman redeemer was one of many sets of rules that came out of the Law of Moses. It is set out mostly in the Old Testament book of Leviticus, chapter 25. If a man owed money but he could not pay it back, he could either sell his land or sell himself or his family into slavery to pay the debt. When that happened, the Law set out the procedure for "redeeming" or buying back the land or the person. To be qualified to act as a redeemer, the person had to be a relative or kinsman. The kinsman had a duty to redeem, to buy back, the enslaved relative or the land that had been sold, if he had enough money to do so. When the kinsman redeemer paid the price to redeem land, his responsibilities did not end there. He had the further obligation to evict or throw out any people who were not on the land lawfully, so that it could be restored to its rightful owner.

Remember that Jehovah had given Adam rulership over the earth. Adam was supposed to act as Jehovah's human representative on earth, and do what Jehovah wanted him to do. But we know that Adam chose to believe the lie of the serpent instead of obeying the Lord. At that point, the serpent (Satan) took over rulership of the world, and the entire world has been under his authority from that time forward. All of mankind, born of Adam, has been born into slavery to Satan, and all of creation is subject to the curse of Adam's Fall as well.

The only way people can get out of this slavery to Satan is to buy our way out. But not one person has the "money" that is required. What is the "money" that is required to buy back a person who in slavery to Satan? Every human being born after Adam is born with a rebellious sin nature. Even before we could speak, we did things that offended Jehovah and are considered sin. And, once a person sins, he deserves death. **The cost of sin is death, the shedding of blood.** What is the cost of redemption, which means the price it takes to buy back a person so that person won't have to die for his own sins? Jehovah set out the **price of our redemption: the blood (meaning the death) of a perfect human being**. Since not one person born after Adam was perfect, because everyone has sinned, we all need a kinsman redeemer who is perfect (and therefore has the "money") to come and buy us back out of slavery. Animal sacrifice will not do. We need a *kinsman*, a *relative*, to die for our sins. We need a perfect human being to die *in our place*.

Hebrews 9:22b ESV
Without the shedding of blood, there is no forgiveness of sins.

Hebrews 9:22b CEV
No sins can be forgiven unless blood is offered.

And now, at last, we have come to the glory of Jehovah's plan!

• 4 •
Why Did Jesus Come? What Is The Message Of The Gospel?

JESUS CAME AS A MAN

Now that we have some understanding of the sad history of human beings, it is time to talk about Jehovah's solution. Since He was the Creator of both the heavenly realm and the earthly realm, He was not caught by surprise when the rebellions occurred. He did not need to crumple up His creation and start over. He had a plan all along to accomplish His desire of having a family in both realms. According to the Bible, this plan existed "before the foundation of the world." This is an expression which means that He knew from the beginning that there would be rebellions and He was prepared to deal with them.

This plan is the means by which we can become members of Jehovah's family. "Before the foundation of the world," the Trinity (God the Father, God the Son, and God the Holy Spirit) had the solution to the evil that would come into the creation when the created beings, both spirit and human, chose not to love their Creator and chose not to obey Him. The solution was that God the Son took on human flesh. He didn't just take on a physical form so that human beings could see Him. He actually became a human being, including being born from a mother like the rest of us. He differed from us, however, in that His Father was Jehovah. Unlike us, He was not a descendant of Adam, and therefore, He did not inherit the sin nature of fallen mankind. Nevertheless, He was still completely human and this is how He, God the Son, Jesus Christ, became the relative of all people on the earth. As a human man, He became our Relative.

As a man, He lived a perfect life in complete submission to the will of His Father. Although He was tempted just as we are, He withstood all temptation to the full. He never gave in to the temptation and thus He never sinned. He kept all the many rules of the Law perfectly. Since He never sinned, He had the "money" to buy sinful people out of slavery. He was our Relative (a human being) and able to pay the price to buy us back. He paid the price of our redemption by dying in our place and that made Him our Redeemer. Philippians 2 says:

> Philippians 2:8 ESV
> *... He humbled Himself by becoming obedient to the point of death, even death on a cross.*

> Philippians 2:8 CEV
> *Christ was humble. He obeyed God and even died on a cross.*

The cross was an extremely cruel way of killing people. His death on a cross was the central part of the plan that the Trinity (God the Father, God the Son, and God the Holy Spirit) had decided upon before He ever created the earth and the people on it. When Jesus Christ, Who never sinned, shed His blood and died on the cross, there was no legal basis for it. That is because He never sinned. Every other human being since Adam has sinned, and we do deserve to die. But He died the death that we deserve to die. He took upon Himself all the sins of all people from the time of Adam until the last person lives, and He paid for them *with His blood*. He laid down His life for us. He died *in our place*. And when He did, God the Father accepted His act of sacrifice as full payment for the redemption of people. He had paid the price necessary to free us from slavery to Satan. The effect is that He bought us for Himself. We belong to Him. Or we *can*, if we choose to do so. We can choose to submit to His authority, to love Him back for all He has done to make it possible for us to live in His kingdom, to be adopted into His family, and to help and assist Him in whatever job He assigns to us.

JESUS ROSE FROM THE DEAD

But there was more! Jesus Christ didn't stay dead! He rose from the dead. This is called resurrection. The Bible says Jesus conquered death! That means that death was overcome. It's as if there had been a battle, and death lost and Jesus won. And in winning, He rescued all of us who live in fear of dying. Remember that death means separation. When Adam and Eve were thrown out of Jehovah's presence, they were separated from their life with Him. In addition to that, from that point on, their bodies grew old and sicknesses afflicted them, and eventually their bodies just died. That death was a separation of the body from the soul and the spirit. The body would decay into dust, but the soul and spirit would then either go directly to Jehovah to be in His presence forever, or, if the person had rejected Jehovah's love, then to a permanent place of separation from Him.

Hebrews 2:14-15 ESV

14Since therefore the children share in flesh and blood, He Himself likewise partook of the same things, that through death He might destroy the one who has the power of death, that is, the devil, 15and deliver all those who through fear of death were subject to lifelong slavery.

Hebrews 2:14-15 CEV

14We are people of flesh and blood. That is why Jesus became one of us. He died to destroy the devil, who had power over death. 15But he also died to rescue all of us who live each day in fear of dying.

Because Jesus Christ rose from the dead, we who love Him and follow Him and obey His commandments can be assured that we, too, will rise from the dead at some time in the future. Our souls and spirits will be placed in a new body that will not have the rebellious sin nature, and will not ever get old or sick or die.

FOLLOWING JESUS

If the payment of Jesus Christ's death was sufficient to buy our redemption, then why is the world still so full of bad things and bad people? The first reason is that people can choose not to believe in the work that Jesus did by dying for them and in their place. They can choose not to love Him, not to want to even know Him, and not to obey His commandments. They are still ruled by their rebellious sin natures, which means that they are still under the authority of Satan. The purchase that Jesus made by dying on the cross and rising to life again does not apply to them because they choose to reject Him. They are not "saved" from having to bear their own punishment for their own sins when their bodies die, because they did not accept the death of Jesus *in their place*. Salvation (being saved) means that you are not just saved *from* having to pay for your own sins, but it also means that you are saved *for* the family life of love and security, forever, in the presence of the Trinity (God the Father, God the Son, and God the Holy Spirit), as well as the presence of all the other people who made the same choice. You are saved *for* the purpose that Jehovah created you: to love Him and enjoy His company forever, and to be His imager, His representative as He governs this world.

CLEARING THE LAND

The second reason that there is still evil in the world is that, while Jesus Christ has beaten Satan and all the evil, fallen angels who work for him, those bad spirit beings still rule this world. It belongs to Jesus Christ, but He will have to force Satan and his followers out because they do not want to admit that they have lost their right to rule this world and everyone in it. Satan and his followers do not want to give up their control over the world and all the people in it who have not believed in and trusted the work of Jesus Christ. And they don't want any people to believe in and trust Jesus, because then those people will no longer be under their control.

Remember that after the kinsman redeemer had bought back the land that his relative had sold to pay off his debts, he still had the duty to throw out any people who might still be on the land, but no longer had the legal right to be there. This last job of our Relative, our Kinsman Redeemer, is in the process of happening now, but will not be complete until sometime in the future. When it is complete, then there will no longer be any bad things or bad people in the world. The Kingdom of God is now here in the world, but it is not here in its fullness yet. But it will be fully here in the world at some time in the future.

And, while we are speaking of this Kingdom of God that will be here in its fullness at some time in the future, this leads us to the last important element of the gospel: Jesus Christ, God the Son, will return to the earthly realm from the heavenly realm at an unknown time in the future. When He comes this second time, He will not come as a baby, born of a mother, like us. Next time, He will erupt out of the unseen, invisible realm, into our visible realm, and the Bible tells us that every person on earth will see Him when He comes (Rev 1:7, 19:11-16, Matt 24:30, Mark 13:26, Luke 21:27). He will come as King of Kings and Lord of Lords, and He will punish all the evil in this earthly realm and also in the invisible, heavenly realm. As our Kinsman Redeemer, He will perform the duty of clearing His land of those who are trespassing on it. He will take all control and rule away from Satan and his fallen angels, and they will be judged and punished.

SUMMARY

Let's summarize the gospel message. One of the three Persons of the Trinity, God the Son, became a human being, born of a human mother just like us. God the Son was known (in English) as Jesus. He lived a perfect life. He never sinned, never made a wrong choice, never did anything bad. Even though He was God, He was also a human being. As a human being, He could die. And He did, taking the punishment that all people deserve for their sins, in their place. Then He rose from the dead, and after spending some time with His followers, He returned to heaven. Soon after that, He sent God the Holy Spirit to those who believed in Him, to help them to make the right choices, and to tell others about Jesus so that they could also be saved from having to pay for their own sins, and from being separated from the presence of Jehovah forever. Those who believe in Jesus, and what He did for us, are "saved." They become members of Jehovah's family by adoption. They are not saved because they were good, or did good things. No one can be good enough or do good enough to earn his way into Jehovah's family. The only One Who could and did do the work of saving us was Jesus Christ.

The final element of the gospel is that Jesus Christ will return to earth at some time in the future, to clear the world of all the evil in it, and to rule over the earth Himself.

Once we are adopted into the family of Jehovah, we should be like the best of families. We should be loyal to one another, take care of one another, love one another, and want the best for all the other family members. When we do these things, we show other people, who are not yet adopted into the family, what it means to be in this family. We also prove to ourselves that we are part of this new family by obeying the rules of the Father of the family, and by loving Him. When we fail, and we will sometimes, we have to tell the truth and admit what we have done. We will always be forgiven, but there may still be some bad consequences if we have hurt someone.

The word "gospel" means good news. What is good about it is that there is nothing we can ever do or be that will make us good enough to be with our Creator. We are less than our Creator. He is perfect. We are not and never will be. You may wonder why that is good news! It is good news because the work of making us good enough has been done *for us*, by Jesus Christ. God the Son became a human being and did it all for us. And He did it because He loves you so much that He wants you to be a part of His forever family. All He asks of you is that you believe Him and show Him your love by obeying His rules.

ONLY TWO CHOICES IN THIS LIFE

Since the time of the Fall of Adam and Eve, people have lived on the earth for a period of time, and then their bodies die. (Enoch and Elijah were the only exceptions.) Death separates the body from the soul and spirit. The body returns to the earth to decay and decompose, but the spirit and soul live on forever. Ecclesiastes 12:7 says that the spirit returns to God Who gave it [life]. This is for the judgment of Jehovah.

Hebrews 9:27 ESV

[I]t is appointed for man to die once, and after that comes judgment.

Hebrews 9:27 CEV

We die only once, and then we are judged.

This one verse alone demolishes the notion of reincarnation. We are given this one life, and what we do in this life will determine how we will spend eternity. Since all people who have lived after Adam (except Jesus Christ) inherited Adam's sin nature, and since people corrupted by sin cannot exist in the presence of a perfect and holy Creator, all people, apart from Jesus Christ, will have to spend eternity away from the presence of their Creator. That sentence may not sound so ominous, until you consider that everything that is good comes from Jehovah. An existence apart from Him is described in the Bible in graphic and terrifying words, such as "outer darkness," where "there shall be weeping and gnashing of teeth" (Matthew 8:12, Matthew 22:13, and Matthew 25:30); a place where the "worm does not die, and the fire is not quenched" (Mark 9:44, 46, and 48); "fiery hell" (Matthew 5:22 and Matthew 18:9); "hell . . . the unquenchable fire" (Mark 9:43); or simply "hell" (Matthew 5:29 and 30, Matthew 10:28, Matthew 23:33, Mark 9:45 and 47, and Luke 12:5). As if this were not scary enough, the Bible states categorically that everyone whose name is not found in the Lamb's Book of Life will be cast into the "lake of fire, which burns with brimstone" (Revelation 19:20 and Revelation 20: 10, 14, and 15). The lake of fire is also described in Revelation 20:14 as the second death, but it is apparently not a death of extinction. There are clear indications that the suffering and the torment of those in the lake of fire goes on forever. Nevertheless, scholars disagree on the length of the duration of hell. What is clear is that it is not a destination to be desired under any circumstances, and the whole point of the message of the gospel is to inform people that hell is the cost of their sin, but because Jesus paid the price for them, they do not have to go there.

Every human being who was born after the Fall of Adam and Eve—except Jesus Christ—is born under the authority and rulership of Satan. It is a life full of sin and emptiness. It is a life with no meaning, no purpose, and no lasting love. It is a life that ends horribly in permanent separation from Jehovah and all that is good. It ends in pain, darkness, loneliness, fear, and suffering forever.

That is why God the Son became a human being and laid down His life in our place, and then rose from the dead: so that, not only are we "saved" from going to hell, to pay for our own sins ourselves, but also we can choose to accept His offer, which is absolutely free, to become part of His life, His family, living under His authority. This is a *new* life, and while it will be a struggle on this earth, it will also be a life full of joy and purpose and meaning and lasting love. And when this life ends, it will be an eternal life of things so wonderful and beautiful that we can't even begin to imagine them. Most of all, we will be all He created us to be, because we will be at home with our heavenly Father and our family.

There are only two choices open to all human beings in this life. You can choose to submit to the authority of Jehovah, Who loves you and will care and provide for you forever. If you do not actively *choose* Him, you will stay where you are, under the authority and rule of Satan, who wants to destroy and kill you. There are no other choices. You will live and die under the authority of one or the other.

<blockquote>
Reject Jesus — you have chosen Satan.
Choose Jesus — you have rejected Satan.
</blockquote>

Those who have rejected Jesus will receive justice. Those who have chosen Jesus will receive mercy.

JEHOVAH IS RECLAIMING THE NATIONS HE ONCE PLACED UNDER THE AUTHORITY OF THE ANGELS (WHO ARE NOW FALLEN ANGELS)

Genesis 12:3 records one of Jehovah's promises to Abraham which is very important to us who were not born as descendants of Abraham. He promised that, through Abraham and the nation Israel that would be formed with his descendants, all the families of the earth would be blessed. Jehovah intended to use the nation Israel to draw all the other nations of the earth back to Himself. When I say, "all the other nations of the earth," I am talking about the descendants of the people at Babel, who rebelled against Him, and didn't want His authority over them. Jehovah would draw them back to a family relationship with Him.

With the perspective of hindsight, we can see now that it was Jesus Who came from the nation of Israel and Who was the means through Whom all the families of the earth would be blessed. "Salvation is from (or out of) the Jews," Jesus said in John 4:22, because it was through a Jew, Jesus, that salvation would become available not just to the nation of Israel, but to all the nations of the world. And all the people of the various nations of the world who believed in, or believe in Jesus Christ, have become children of Abraham, just as if they were his physical descendants. That means that all the blessings that were promised to Abraham can belong to those who believe, too.

Galatians 3:26-29 NASB
²⁶For you are all sons of God through faith in Christ Jesus. ²⁷For all of you who were baptized into Christ have clothed yourselves with Christ. ²⁸There is neither Jew nor Greek, there is neither slave nor free man, there is neither male nor female; for you are all one in

*Christ Jesus. ²⁹And **if you belong to Christ, then you are Abraham's offspring**, heirs according to promise.*

Galatians 3:26-29 CEV

*²⁶All of you are God's children because of your faith in Christ Jesus. ²⁷And when you were baptized, it was as though you had put on Christ in the same way you put on new clothes. ²⁸Faith in Christ Jesus is what makes each of you equal with each other, whether you are a Jew or a Greek, a slave or a free person, a man or a woman. ²⁹So **if you belong to Christ, you are now part of Abraham's family**, and you will be given what God has promised.*

In the New Testament, in Matthew chapter 16, Jesus asked His followers what they thought about Him. He wanted to know if they understood that He was God the Son, Who had become a human man just like them. One of them, named Peter, had understood.

Matthew 16:15-18 ESV

¹⁵He said to them, "But who do you say that I am?" ¹⁶Simon Peter replied, "You are the Christ, the Son of the living God." ¹⁷And Jesus answered him, "Blessed are you, Simon Bar-Jonah! For flesh and blood has not revealed this to you, but My Father who is in heaven. ¹⁸And I tell you, you are Peter, and on this rock I will build My church, and the gates of hell shall not prevail against it."

Matthew 16:15-18 BBE (Bible in Basic English)

¹⁵He says to them, "But who do you say that I am?" ¹⁶And Simon Peter made answer and said, "You are the Christ, the Son of the living God." ¹⁷And Jesus made answer and said to him, "A blessing on you, Simon Bar-Jonah: because this knowledge has not come to you from flesh and blood, but from My Father in heaven. ¹⁸And I say to you that you are Peter, and on this rock will My church be based, and the doors of hell will not overcome it."

The Greek word that is translated as "hell" is "hades," the place of the souls of the dead. The location in which the exchange between Jesus and Peter took place was Caesarea-Philippi, at the foot of Mount Hermon. This location, Mount Hermon, was considered to be the "gates of hell," the gateway to the realm of the dead. Moreover, the Jews believed that Mount Hermon was the location where the sons of God of Genesis 6 had come down to mate with the human women, resulting in the hybrid race of the Nephilim. In this context, what Jesus was declaring was that *He* was the rightful owner of this world and of the people in it who were under Satan's control, and He had come to take it and them back. He was declaring war on Satan and all the fallen angels. He was also going to take back the nations which Jehovah had assigned to the care and authority of the "sons of God" who had at one time been good angels, but who had let the power of watching over the nations (other than Israel) corrupt them and make them evil. Jesus was God in a human body, and He had come to let people know that He loved them and He was going to make as many as would join Him a part of His family. Jehovah had started by creating the nation of Israel, and when the people of Israel had failed to love Him back as they should have, Jesus came as a human man to show people Who God is and how much He wanted them in His family. He would begin with the Jews, but He was going to get a family from all the other nations, too.

After Jesus died and rose from the dead, He stayed with His followers for a while, and then He left to return to His home in the spiritual realm, with God the Father. The Bible says that He ascended into heaven. But shortly after He left, He sent God the Holy Spirit, the third Person of the Trinity, in His place. Unlike Jesus (God the Son), Who became a human being, God the Holy Spirit is now, and always has been, a Spirit. But, because He is a Spirit, He has the ability to live inside us. From there, He can speak to our minds in our thoughts, and He can guide us to make the right choices. He helps us to overcome our rebellious sinful natures that will always make the wrong choices.

When we choose to believe that Jesus is the Son of God, God the Son, and that He died in our place for our sins; when we choose to accept His redeeming payment that buys us out of slavery to Satan and sin; when we agree to live under His authority and to love Him and keep His commandments— that is the time of our salvation. And at that time, God the Holy Spirit comes to live within us. We will not hear or understand His way of "speaking" to us at first. For most people, it takes a long time of studying the Bible and praying and learning to listen before we can recognize His voice. It is not a voice you can hear with your ears. Usually what happens is that you are reading the Bible, and some words or a sentence or a few sentences will suddenly be very clear, as if you are seeing them for the first time, or just understanding them for the first time. This is His primary way of communicating with us. That means, of course, that you have to spend lots of time reading the Bible, because it is the only way you can get to know the Trinity, and His ways and His usual responses, and, most importantly, His amazing love. After all, this is about a family relationship, with a perfect Father Who loves you more than even your human mother and father do (or did), and Who knows what is best for you, and will help you to be all that He created you to be.

PART TWO
THE LIFE OF A CHRISTIAN

LIVING IN THE TRUTH

There are two words in the life of a Christian that we need to make sure we understand. The first is truth. Jehovah created all that exists. He created all the laws of mathematics and science, like physics, biology, and chemistry, and specific things like magnetism, electricity, and gravity. He designed and created our human bodies, which worked perfectly before the Fall of Adam and Eve. He designed and created every plant and animal. He set up the delicate balance of a perfect ecosystem that would support the life of the plants, animals and human beings He created. He set the stars and planets on their courses. Unfortunately, the Fall of man affected all of the created order as well as human beings, so there is a lot of violence in nature and out in space as well, but Jehovah will set that all straight at some time in the future.

The point here is that all things that exist, whether the spirit realm, which is invisible to us, or the earthly realm, which we can see, are governed by Jehovah. All reality (what is real, whether we can see it or not) is determined by Him, and measured against the absolute standard of His truth. There is an absolute truth, and Jehovah (well, the whole Trinity) *is* that Truth. Everything the Trinity is, and says, and does, is truth. The Creator is the fixed, immovable standard of what is true. You cannot determine what is true by your feelings or emotions or your mind, because all of those change regularly. For example, we change our minds about something when we learn more about that something. But Jehovah already knows everything, so He is not going to learn something He didn't know and then change the truth about what He created. And, for goodness' sake, do not listen to anyone who tells you to follow your heart! Because of the Fall, we have been corrupted in our bodies, souls (our "hearts"), and spirits.

> Jeremiah 17:9 KJV
> *The heart is deceitful above all things, and desperately wicked: who can know it?*

> Jeremiah 17:9 ESV
> *The heart is deceitful above all things, and desperately sick; who can understand it?*

> Jeremiah 17:9 CEV
> You people of Judah are so deceitful that you even fool yourselves, and you can't change.

You can never trust yourself to determine what is true and what is a lie. The only way you can know whether something is true is by comparing it to what Jehovah has told us in the Bible. That is the definitive Word to us.

Jehovah does not lie. He *never* lies. In fact, He *cannot* lie (Numbers 23:19, 1 Samuel 15:29, Titus 1:2, Hebrews 6:18).

Just as Jehovah cannot lie, Satan and the fallen angels cannot tell the truth. If one of them speaks, you can be certain that it is not the truth. There may be a small kernel of truth in there, but it will be distorted or wrapped in a lie. You can never trust Satan or the fallen angels, because it is their nature to lie.

> John 8:44 ESV
> *You are of your father the devil, and your will is to do your father's desires. He was a murderer from the beginning, and has nothing to do with the truth, because **there is no truth in him**. When he lies, he speaks out of his own character, for he is a liar and the father of lies.*

> John 8:44 CEV
> *Your father is the devil, and you do exactly what he wants. He has always been a murderer and a liar. There is nothing truthful about him. He speaks on his own, and **everything he says is a lie**. Not only is he a liar himself, but he is also the father of all lies.*

Everything that is **true** and **right** has been determined by Jehovah alone. Everything that is not in line with what Jehovah has said is a **lie** and **wrong**. It doesn't matter if all your friends say something is right, or if the whole of America says something is right. If what they are saying is different from what Jehovah says in the Bible, then Jehovah is right and everyone else — all your friends, and the whole of America — is wrong. **Truth is Jehovah's view of a matter**. It is as simple as that. And, if you are standing up for the side of Jehovah, it is as difficult as that.

The hard part is recognizing the lies. Satan will distort reality by getting you to change your focus. For example, he will take some need you have, or some insecurity, and he will get you to question whether Jehovah, Who is your heavenly Father, loves you after all, and really cares for you. When you question whether He loves you or cares for you, you have already believed a lie. You must be convinced of the truth that Jehovah loves you so much that God the Son became a human being and died a horrible death just so that you could be adopted into His family. *Nothing* that anyone says can change that truth. Never doubt that truth.

Now, it may seem as if I am changing the subject, but I am just stopping for a minute to give you an example. Let's say you invented a board game. You would decide everything about the playing of that game. You would decide the rules of that game. If someone playing the game doesn't like your rules, he could try to cheat, which would defeat the whole point of the game.

In a similar way, the rules of our lives on earth have also been created by Jehovah. We can try to cheat or get around the rules, but we will always get hurt, and we will often hurt others as well. If you think about it, cheating is really rather stupid. Jehovah knows absolutely everything. He even knows our hearts and our intentions better than we do. Do we really think we can do anything without His knowing all about it? We have to live according to the rules set out by our Creator. We have to live in accordance with the truths that He has set out in the Bible. Our thoughts and our words and our actions must line up with His truth.

In addition, as the Creator of the people and the earth they live in, He has the right to decide what the rules of living will be. He decides what is right and what is wrong. If a person disagrees with a decision that Jehovah has made, he should not expect to speak to Him on equal footing. A person is only a created being, imperfect and unable to understand all that Jehovah knows. We have no right to disagree with Him on any point on which He has stated His position.

As an example, let's imagine that there is a person who has been taught that there is a law of gravity. If you hold a breakable china cup in your hand, and you let go of it, it will fall to the ground, and shatter into pieces. We know from experience that the cup will not fly upward or sideways. It will simply fall down to the ground. But this person in our example chooses not to believe in the law of gravity. "That may be *your* truth," says he to you, "but it is not *my* truth." And to prove that he doesn't believe in the law of gravity, he walks off the edge of a roof of a tall building. What do you think will happen to him? Will he continue to walk on air? Or perhaps he will float up heavenward? No, you know that he will fall to the ground and splatter just as the china cup would. It doesn't matter whether you believe in the law of gravity or not. It doesn't matter how *sincerely* you believe or not. The law of gravity exists. And it is the same with Jehovah and the beings He created who exist in the heavenly realm, both good and bad. Someone will say he doesn't believe in the existence of Jehovah or of the devil or demons or angels. And he may live his life based on that unbelief, telling you that such beings are not part of *his* truth. In the end, he will find out the hard way, just as the roof-walker did, that some *truths* exist, whether you believe in them or not. There is absolute truth. That absolute truth has been revealed to us in the Person of Jesus Christ. The sooner we adjust our living to the truth, the better off we will be.

FAITH

The second word in the life of a Christian that we need to understand is faith. As I said in an earlier section, faith means you believe that what Jehovah says is true. The Bible defines faith in slightly different words.

> Hebrews 11:1 and 6 ESV
> ¹*Now faith is the assurance of things hoped for, the conviction of things not seen....⁶And without faith it is impossible to please Him, for whoever would draw near to God must believe that He exists and that He rewards those who seek Him.*

> Hebrews 11:1 and 6 CEV
> ¹*Faith makes us sure of what we hope for and gives us proof of what we cannot see...⁶But without faith no one can please God. We must believe that God is real and that He rewards everyone who searches for Him.*

If we understand that faith means that you believe what Jehovah says is true, then it makes sense when the Bible says that you have to have faith before you can please Him. Think about the relationship you had with your parents when you were a child. They would not have been pleased if you didn't believe what they told you! It is the same with your relationship with your heavenly Father. (Remember that being a Christian, a follower of Jesus, means that you are adopted into His family.) He expects you to believe Him when He tells you something in the Bible. He will never lie to you, because He always and only speaks the truth. If He says in the Bible that He will correct you when you do something wrong (Hebrews 12:5-11), you can believe He will, although it may not be in the time that you expect. If He says that He loves you with an everlasting love (Jeremiah 31:3), then you can believe He means exactly what He says there, too.

PRAYER

Prayer is a word that describes our communication with Jehovah/Jesus/God the Holy Spirit. This communication goes both ways, from us to Him and from Him to us. Usually, He "speaks" by making a Bible passage we are reading seem to jump out at us, or by helping us to understand a passage that we were confused about. For our part, we can and should tell Him everything that is on our minds. You can speak to Him out loud or in your mind, but, if you are alone, it is best to speak out loud because your mind is less likely to wander. It is true that He already knows our minds and what we are thinking, but He has created us and designed us to speak to Him. He wants us to be in a relationship with Him.

What are we supposed to say to Him in prayer? The answer is anything and everything that you are thinking about or puzzled about or happy about or worried about. The important thing to remember about prayer is that it should always be the *first* act when you are troubled about something. Turning to Jehovah in prayer should be your first response in all circumstances, because only He knows exactly what happened, down to the last detail. There is nothing wrong with talking to mature and godly people after that, so long as you remember that they are not Jehovah/Jesus/the Holy Spirit.

There are some specific things you should pray about. We know that, every day, we do or say or think things that are not nice. Even if you have not studied the Bible very much yet, you know when you have hurt someone else's feelings, or when you have been angry because you didn't get what you wanted. In your prayers, it is important to confess the things that you have thought or said or done that you know were wrong. To confess means simply to agree with. You are agreeing with your Creator that you should not have thought or said or done what you did. And then you ask Him to forgive you. Of course, you should intend to do better tomorrow, and to ask for God the Holy Spirit to help you the next time you are in the same or similar situation. This is what repentance is. To repent means to turn away from something bad, and to turn instead toward Jehovah. We should live our lives in constant confession and repentance, as God the Holy Spirit teaches us what is not pleasing to our adoptive Father.

The most common aspect of prayer that people think of is called petition. This means asking Jehovah for something you need. The Bible says that He knows our needs before we do, but He still requires us to ask for what we need before He will provide it. He will never force anything on us, even good things.

Matthew 6:8b ESV and CEV
[Y]our Father knows what you need before you ask Him.

James 4:2b ESV
You do not have, because you do not ask.

James 4:2b CEV
But you still cannot get what you want, and you won't get it by fighting and arguing. You should pray for it.

Philippians 4:19 ESV
And my God will supply every need of yours according to His riches in glory in Christ Jesus.

Philippians 4:19 CEV
I pray that God will take care of all your needs with the wonderful blessings that come from Christ Jesus!

Of course, this does not mean that you will be given every single thing you ask for. Sometimes, we ask for things that we think we want, but

Jehovah knows that we are not ready to handle that thing, or it would get in the way of our growing spiritually, so He does not grant it.

Prayer is much more than asking Jehovah for something you need or want. It also means thanking Him for all the good things in your life. The list could be as long and detailed as you like, but here are a few you could thank Him for every day:
- that the Most High God, Who created you and your human family, has loved you so much that He has made it possible for you to be adopted forever into His family. That's a huge gift!
- that Jesus rose from the dead, which made it possible for you to be moved out from under the rule of Satan and into the household of Jesus.

In addition to thanking Him for all the good things in your life, prayer includes praising Jehovah for all His wonderful qualities. As you study your Bible, you will learn more of them, but here are a few of them:
- that He is good. All things that are good, like warm sunshine on a spring day, and rain in the summer, or a beautiful sunset, are from Him. He is the Source of all happiness and joy. He is the Source of all life, including yours!
- that He is love. His love is perfect, and much greater than we can possibly imagine.
- that He is perfect. He never makes a wrong choice or a mistake.
- that He is just. He will punish all evil and bad, if not now, then at some time in the future. You can rest assured that evil people and fallen angels will not ever get past Him. They will get exactly what they deserve. He will see to it.
- that He is in control, even when it seems that the world has gone crazy. There are times when He allows evil to rule, but He will always use it for the good of His people. Genesis 50:20 (CEV) quotes a man named Joseph saying, "You tried to harm me, but God made it turn out for the best."

There is another important aspect of prayer: intercession. This is difficult to understand, but for reasons only Jehovah knows, He has chosen to use our prayers to accomplish His desires. Because He is the Most

High God, and the Creator of all that exists, He could clearly do anything He wanted, without any help from the good angels or from us human beings. But He has chosen to allow us to help Him. In fact, there are some things He could do, but will not do, until we participate. And prayer is one major way in which we participate. When we pray, He causes things to happen not just in the earthly realm, but also in the heavenly realm. When we pray for His will to be done on earth as it is in heaven, we are actually, in some unknown way, helping Him to accomplish His will on earth as it is done in heaven.

And there is more. Next we'll talk about spiritual warfare. Prayer is a major part of spiritual warfare. Our prayers affect what happens in the spiritual realm. Our prayers can arm the good angels and give them strength to do their job. And our prayers can also bind up the fallen angels and actually stop them from the harm they mean to cause in the earthly realm. The Bible tells us that Satan puts a sort of blindfold over the eyes of people who don't know Jesus, so that they cannot see or understand the message of the gospel, and be adopted into Jehovah's family. 2 Corinthians 4:4 ESV says that "the god of this world [that's Satan] has blinded the minds of the unbelievers, to keep them from seeing the light of the gospel of the glory of Christ, who is the image of God." Our prayers can stop Satan and his fallen angels from blinding these people, so that, when we speak of Jesus to them, they are able to see and hear and understand. Do our prayers matter? Yes, more than we can possibly know.

SPIRITUAL WARFARE

Your *faith in the truth* will be tested from the time you submit yourself to the authority of Jesus Christ to the end of your life in this world. Being a follower of Jesus and an adopted member of Jehovah's family means that you will face some hard times in your life in this world. Jesus told His followers that, since the world hated Him, those in the world will hate His followers, too.

Luke 6:22-23 ESV

²²Blessed are you when people hate you and when they exclude you and revile you and spurn your name as evil, on account of the Son of Man! ²³Rejoice in that day, and leap for joy, for behold, your reward is great in heaven; for so their fathers did to the prophets.

Luke 6:22-23 CEV

²²God will bless you when others hate you and won't have anything to do with you. God will bless you when people insult you and say cruel things about you, all because you are a follower of the Son of Man. ²³Long ago your own people did these same things to the prophets. So when this happens to you, be happy and jump for joy! You will have a great reward in heaven.

John 15:18-19 ESV

¹⁸If the world hates you, know that it has hated Me before it hated you. ¹⁹If you were of the world, the world would love you as its own; but because you are not of the world, but I chose you out of the world, therefore the world hates you.

John 15:18-19 CEV

¹⁸If the people of this world hate you, just remember that they hated Me first. ¹⁹If you belonged to the world, its people would love you. But you don't belong to the world. I have chosen you to leave the world behind, and that is why its people hate you.

1 John 3:13 ESV

Do not be surprised, brothers, that the world hates you.

1 John 3:13 CEV

My friends, don't be surprised if the people of this world hate you.

Why is this so? Why does the world hate Jesus and His family? Because the world is still ruled by Satan and the fallen angels. Remember that Jesus has already won the battle against Satan and the fallen angels. Jesus won when He died and rose from the dead. But Satan and his fallen angels won't admit that they have lost and they don't want you to know that they have lost. So, until Jesus throws them out— and He will in the future, because that is what a Kinsman Redeemer does— Satan is still the "god of this world," according to 2 Corinthians 4:4. Satan and his fallen angels do not want to lose even one of their slaves to the freedom they will have with Jesus and His family. The fallen angels will do everything they can to make you decide that you made a bad choice and you need to come back to them. Of course, we know that lying is the only language they speak. They cannot speak the truth because it is their nature to lie. And they will say whatever lie they can think of to hook your attention and get you back into their world.

Another reason why the world is a difficult place to live in is that what happens in the spiritual realm affects the earthly realm. Remember that the two realms are connected. While the events in one realm affect the other, the invisible heavenly supernatural realm is the controlling reality. The real power and authority exist in that realm. What happens there affects our seen world, the natural world, more powerfully than so-called "natural" events. That is why Jehovah provided us with a supernatural weapon: His Word, the Bible. There is a war going on in the spiritual realm *all the time* over every human being that is alive. Satan and his fallen angels want to destroy you, body, soul, and spirit. But they don't want you to know what they are doing because they can work much better and with more success if you don't fight them. And if you don't know they are out to hurt you, you won't fight them.

Because of this battle in the heavenly realm, Jehovah warned us in Ephesians not to be fooled by what we think is happening in the earthly realm. The real battle is in the spiritual realm.

> Ephesians 6:12 ESV
> *For we do not wrestle against flesh and blood, but against the rulers, against the authorities, against the cosmic powers over this present darkness, against the spiritual forces of evil in the heavenly places.*

> Ephesians 6:12 CEV
> *We are not fighting against humans. We are fighting against forces and authorities and against rulers of darkness and powers in the spiritual world.*

The "rulers of darkness and powers in the spiritual world" are the fallen angels. They will do anything they can to keep you from understanding, accepting, and being adopted into the family of Jehovah. As an example, you may feel that you should take your Bible off the shelf and read it. The demons who are around you will immediately "speak" to your mind and you will find yourself thinking, "I don't really feel like that now. Besides, I have other things I would rather do." The first and most important thing a human being needs to do is to read the Bible every day. It is more important than the food you need to stay alive. It is more important because the words in the Bible are the "food" that will keep you alive in eternity.

> Deuteronomy 32:47 ESV
> *For it [the Word of the Lord] is no empty word for you, but **your very life**, and by this word you shall live long in the land that you are going over the Jordan to possess.*

> Deuteronomy 32:47 CEV
> *The Law isn't empty words. It can give you a long life in the land that you are going to take.*

Deuteronomy 8:3 ESV

*And He humbled you and let you hunger and fed you with manna, which you did not know, nor did your fathers know, that He might make you know that **man does not live by bread alone, but man lives by every word that comes from the mouth of the Lord.***

Deuteronomy 8:3b CEV

*The Lord was teaching you that **people need more than food to live-they need every word that the Lord has spoken.***

Jesus quoted this passage in Deuteronomy when He was tempted by the devil, when He was fasting from food and was hungry:

Matthew 4:3-4 ESV

*³And the tempter came and said to Him, "If you are the Son of God, command these stones to become loaves of bread." ⁴But He answered, "It is written, '**Man shall not live by bread alone, but by every word that comes from the mouth of God.**'"*

Matthew 4:3-4 CEV

*³Then the devil came to him and said, "If you are God's Son, tell these stones to turn into bread." ⁴Jesus answered, "The Scriptures say: '**No one can live only on food. People need every word that God has spoken.**'"*

You will find that you will have to fight what feels like resistance inside you. You will have to discipline yourself to make yourself do what you need to do for your very survival eternally. It is in the regular, ongoing reading and studying of the Bible that you develop a relationship with the Father of your new family. If you cannot make the time to spend with Him in this world, then you should not be surprised if He will not want to spend any time with you in the eternity that comes after this life.

In addition to building the best relationship you will ever have, ever, the time you spend reading your Bible, and growing up in Christ, will make you accustomed to handling the truth. It is only by knowing the truth that you will be able to recognize a lie, and the more you know of the truth, the better you will be able to spot even a little lie.

This battle that is going on in the spiritual realm will show up in the earthly realm most often in your mind. You will need to guard your thoughts. In order to do that, you have to stay aware of your thoughts. When you think something, you need to notice whether it is a good thought or a bad thought. The more you practice taking control of your bad thoughts and replacing them with good ones, the faster you will grow in your spirit. This is called self-control, and it is one segment of the fruit of the Holy Spirit.

> Galatians 5:22-23 ESV
> *²²But the fruit of the Spirit is love, joy, peace, patience, kindness, goodness, faithfulness, ²³gentleness, **self-control**; against such things there is no law.*

> Galatians 5:22-23 CEV
> ²²God's Spirit makes us loving, happy, peaceful, patient, kind, good, faithful, ²³gentle, and **self-controlled**. There is no law against behaving in any of these ways.

Satan and his fallen angels are not the only source of problems as we try to live our lives in a way that honors our heavenly Father. Even though the spirit part of us is renewed and saved from eternal separation from Jehovah, our rebellious sin nature will still trip us up on a regular basis. This is so because we still want to do what we want to do; and we want to do what we want to do *when* we want to do it! It is very annoying when someone in authority over us tells us to do something we don't want to do or to stop doing what we want to do! The Bible talks about this problem, too.

James 1:14-15 ESV

^{14}But each person is tempted when he is lured and enticed by his own desire. ^{15}Then desire, when it has conceived, gives birth to sin, and sin when it is fully grown brings forth death.

James 1:14-15 CEV

^{14}We are tempted by our own desires that drag us off and trap us. ^{15}Our desires make us sin, and when sin is finished with us, it leaves us dead.

These verses are telling us that we are very good at coming up with our own ideas of ways to have fun that our heavenly Father knows are bad for us. For that reason, He has told us that, when we do those things, that is sin. What we need to remember is that we can *think* of things that Jehovah calls sin, and we must control those thoughts, too. If we allow ourselves to keep thinking about those forbidden things, we will allow ourselves to be trapped in that sin, and that can drag us further and further away from Jehovah. This is why we have to be very careful to monitor at all times what thoughts are going on in our minds. This is a life-long skill, and everyone has to work on it constantly to get better at it.

There is an incentive to help us as we work on monitoring our thoughts. It is to remember that whatever it is that Jehovah has defined as sin has wrath built into it. Put another way, sin has consequences built into it. Remember the soccer game we talked about in the section on The Cost of Sin? When the players observed the rules, fewer people got hurt. When they did not, there were more injuries. The injuries were the natural consequence of not playing by the rules. That is a picture of sin. The injurious consequences to you and to others are built into the sin itself.

One very helpful point to remember is that, as you fight these spiritual battles in your mind, you are not fighting *for* a victory. You are really fighting *from* victory. Jesus Christ has already defeated Satan and all his fallen angels. They just have not admitted that they lost. And they are hoping that *you* won't know that they have lost, because then they can try to convince you that you cannot beat them. The truth is that you don't have to beat them. Jesus Christ already did that. Your job is to remember that and to *stand firm* in His victory. Toss out those negative thoughts the minute they come into your mind. Remind yourself instead that you are a child of the Most High God and you belong to Jesus Christ because He paid for you with His very life. Furthermore, once you have accepted Jesus Christ as the Lord of your life, God the Holy Spirit comes to live in your heart and mind, and He will help to teach you and guide you and make you stronger in your spiritual walk. As a human being, you do not have the strength to deal with fallen angels. But as a child of the Most High God, you can and must stand firm in the authority and power and strength of Jesus Christ, which is unimaginably greater than that of any created being, even Satan.

PREPARING FOR THE RETURN OF JESUS CHRIST

A very important part of the gospel message is that Jesus, Who is now in the heavenly realm with Jehovah, will return to the earth in the future. When He comes, He will come thundering out of heaven and every person alive on the earth at that time will see Him. It will be impossible to miss.

Revelation 1:7 ESV
He is coming with the clouds, and every eye will see Him…

Revelation 1:7 CEV
He is coming with the clouds. Everyone will see Him.

When He came the first time, He was born, like us, from a human mother, and grew from a baby to a little boy, to a teenage boy, and then to a man. The next time He comes, He will come as the man who ascended into heaven after His death and resurrection. He will come as the Ruler and King, because that is exactly what He is! When He comes, He will deal out justice to all the evil both in this world and in the unseen heavenly realm.

> Isaiah 24:21 ESV
> *On that day the Lord will punish the host of heaven, in heaven, and the kings of the earth, on the earth.*

> Isaiah 24:21 AMP (Amplified Bible)
> *And in that day the Lord will visit and punish the host of the high ones on high [the host of heaven in heaven, celestial beings] and the kings of the earth on the earth.*

Before He comes, however, the world will have become terribly evil, and life will be very hard for those of us whom He has adopted into His family. When Jesus was on earth the first time, He described what the earth would be like when He comes the second time. He said it would be the same as it was before the time of the Noahic flood, the flood in the time of Noah. Let's compare what was happening in the world just before the flood with the world today.

Genesis 6 begins with the description of spirit beings in the heavenly realms (all of whom we are calling "angels" for now) who were attracted to the beautiful human women on earth. So some of these angels took on human form, and went to earth and had children with these women. The children were hybrids; they were half human and half spirit being. They were called the Nephilim in the book of Genesis.

Another result of this direct intervention from the unseen spirit realm into our world, the seen realm, was that evil in all forms spread rapidly among people. The fallen angels taught the human beings things that they were not meant to know, things that were evil. It was the same problem that Adam and Eve had had. People chose to believe the lies of the fallen, evil spiritual beings, instead of the truth of Jehovah. The result was that there was a very fast decline in the morals of human beings. People began to do all kinds of horrible things to each other that Jehovah had specifically forbidden. They cheated; they lied; they were violent toward one another; they stole from one another; they killed one another; and there were all kinds of sexual corruption and perversion. Instead of sex being only between a man and a woman who were married to each other, people had sex with others to whom they were not married, and men began to have sex with other men instead of with women, and women did the same with other women. Worst of all, the adults began to have sex with children.

These two things are the key characteristics of the times before the Noahic flood: (1) direct intervention in this world by fallen spiritual beings; and (2) evil behavior among people that became so widespread that it was accepted as "normal." The relatively few people who did not fall for the corrupt ways that most people accepted were humiliated, laughed at, hated, rejected, and ostracized. Just imagine how alone Noah must have felt during the long time that he was building the ark. His neighbors must have pointed at him and made fun of him. Cruel jokes would have centered around Noah; and close friends would have backed away.

Today, we are very close to the same state of affairs in our country. There is evil and corruption everywhere, and all forms of sexual perversion are held up as admirable. People are self-centered, selfish, childish, cruel, quick to judge, mean-spirited, and lazy. They want only to be entertained, and almost all entertainment available today brainwashes people. By that I mean that the entertainment gets people to accept all the lies of Satan and his fallen angels, and to reject all that is of Jehovah. In television shows and movies, those who are following Jesus Christ are mocked and laughed at as narrow-minded, bigoted haters.

This widespread depravity was one of the two key characteristics of the times of Noah. The other was the entry of the fallen angels into this world. Remember that they took on the physical form of men, so we don't know just how much the human beings living at that time knew. Did people know at once that these "men" were not really human beings? Or did they understand only after the strange children, the giant Nephilim, were born to the women? The same questions apply today.

Fallen angels also came to this world after the Noahic flood. We know this for two reasons, both of which come straight out of the Bible. The first is that Genesis 6:4 says so explicitly:

Genesis 6:4 ESV
*The Nephilim were on the earth in those days [before the flood], and **also afterward**, when the sons of God came in to the daughters of man and they bore children to them.*

Genesis 6:4 CEV
*The children of the supernatural beings who had married these women...were called Nephilim and lived on the earth at that time [before the flood] **and even later.***

The second is that there are many references later in the Old Testament to the presence of the giant Nephilim on the earth after the flood. Here are some of them:
- the Hebrews were afraid of the Nephilim, and didn't want to enter the land that Jehovah promised them (Numbers 13:33);
- when the Hebrews entered the land, Jehovah commanded them to kill all the people in specific areas, which were the areas where the Nephilim (also called Anakim and Rephaim) lived. One example is in Deuteronomy 3:11, which describes the huge bed of Og, "of the remnant of the Rephaim;"
- Moses told the second generation of Hebrews about the travels of their parents, and he told them about the Anakim and Rephaim and Emim (who were called the Nephilim in Genesis).
- Goliath, whom young David killed, is described as a giant man (1 Samuel 17:4-7);
- David fought other battles against descendants of the giants (1 Chronicles 20).

These are just some examples that tell us that the hybrid, half-human, half-celestial beings were again on the earth after the Noahic flood.

Since Jesus said that the times before His second coming to the earth will be like the times of Noah, it is implied that there will be another invasion of fallen celestial beings on this earth. Will we know who they are? It is possible, perhaps, that they would pretend to be aliens from another planet. Or else they could just take on human form and we won't know that they are any different from the normal human beings. But we can be watchful for signs of super-human abilities, like the Marvel heroes have.

And now I have to tell you the hardest thing about living in the times shortly before the return of Jesus to the earth.

We are told in the book of Revelation that there will be an unusually evil man who will rule over all the earth before Jesus returns. In the book of Revelation, he is called the beast and the "first" beast. People refer to him as the antichrist, because he will be completely against Jesus Christ, and he will also want to take the place of Jesus Christ. Most people think that Jehovah alone possesses supernatural powers, and therefore any supernatural "sign and wonder" must be attributable to Him. But, while Satan and other celestial beings, who were created by Jehovah, are not as powerful as Jehovah, he and they also possess supernatural powers. Satan will invest the antichrist with his supernatural powers, and, as a result, the antichrist will fool almost all the people on the earth into thinking that He is God Himself. He will be very, very good at fooling people, and it will be hard for even those of us who follow Jesus to know who he is. Those who don't know Jesus won't even know they are being deceived.

One of the things the antichrist will require everyone to do is to take a particular mark on their right hand or on their forehead. The Bible calls this "the mark of the beast." At this time, no one knows what that mark will be. Right now there are people who are implanting little chips into their hands, so they don't have to carry around keys to their offices and homes. It is possible that someday soon, all people will be told they have to have a chip implanted with all their medical information so that, if someone is in a car accident, the police and firemen and ambulance EMTs will be able to get the necessary medical information about a person who is unconscious and can't talk. The next step, which is also already possible, is to have all of each person's financial information on an implanted chip. Then, when anyone goes to the grocery store, they could pay for their food by putting their hand over the scanner, instead of paying with cash or a credit card.

Since technology changes so fast, it is possible that the mark of the beast will not be a chip which is implanted into your right hand or forehead, but may instead be a form of a tattoo which has information imbedded into it. Or perhaps it will be a time-release capsule injected into the hand that, like a vaccine, promises to end all human illness and aging, but instead actually changes a person's DNA so that he or she is, like the Nephilim, no longer fully human, and is therefore no longer capable of being redeemed by the blood of Jesus Christ. Or it may be something entirely different. No one knows right now. What we can know, however, is that it will be, at a minimum, a mark of allegiance. Satan always counterfeits whatever Jehovah has done. The antichrist's mark on the forehead or right hand copies the phylacteries the Hebrews wore on their foreheads and wrists to declare their allegiance and loyalty to Jehovah and His word (Exodus 13:9, 16; Deuteronomy 6:5-8).

This antichrist will also require everyone to bow down to him and worship him as God. As an adopted child of the Most High God, there are three things you must ***never, never*** do. One is that you must never allow anyone to put any kind of a mark onto or into your hand or forehead. Since we do not know at this time what the mark will be, the key words to remember are "right hand" and "forehead." Do not allow anyone to put any mark in or on either of those two places.

The second thing you must never do is to bow down to and worship this antichrist. Since the two requirements will be related, they will probably both be required at the same time. That means that anyone who requires everyone to have a mark on their right hand or on their forehead will be the one you must never bow down to and worship as God.

The third thing is that you must never deny that Jesus Christ is LORD. He is God Almighty, and, if you have submitted your life to Him, He is your LORD. No matter what is done to you or your loved ones, do not deny Him. If you are a mother of young children, do not think that Jehovah will allow you to deny Jesus for the sake of your little ones. He will not. During this unspeakably horrific time, we can be sure that we will all be dying very soon, including our children, whether we deny Him or not. Do not think that your sacrifice will save them; it will not. If your little ones are old enough to understand even a little, teach them to claim Jesus as LORD. All that matters is keeping our *faith in the truth* of the One Who has the power to destroy our souls and spirits in hell. We can know that our suffering and the suffering of our children will not last forever. Jesus will rescue us either by the death of our bodies (but not our souls and spirits!) or by His physical return. In either case, it will be soon after the requirement of the mark is imposed. At this time, my thinking is that the horror will not last more than three and a half years.

For most of the world, taking the mark and worshiping the antichrist will be just the next step in technology. Most people will go on buying and selling, and living and working. For them, life will go on in the new "normal." In contrast, our refusal to take the mark and to bow down to the antichrist will mean that we will be treated as Noah was, only much worse. We will not be able to buy food or medicine. Children may be separated from their parents, and many of us will be killed. All of us who follow Christ may be sent to camps the way the Nazis rounded up the Jews in World War 2, and we may have to face the same horrors the Jews did then. This is a terrifying thought to all of us, to parents as well as to children. But we have to remember that Jehovah is allowing this dreadful evil for His purposes, and we can't begin to understand them. What we can know is that He will take what was intended for evil and He will use it for our good and for His glory. I repeat: what we must do is to hang onto our *faith in the truth*, because the worst thing evil can do to us is to kill the body. But Jehovah will preserve and save our souls and spirits and He will have great rewards for those of us who stay faithful to Him until we die.

If we are the ones who are alive in the days of the antichrist, then we will live in the most difficult time of all human history. But Jehovah knows exactly what He is doing, and *He chose you to live in this particular time*. It will be a time of very hard testing, but He knows that you will get through it, even if you die, *so long as you depend on Him and His strength*. Remind yourself of what you learned in the earlier section on spiritual warfare. Your real enemy will not be the antichrist, or the people who work for him. Your real enemy is Satan and the fallen angels who work for him. They have to have a human body to work through, and they will be the ones who are causing all the trouble. Here is a passage from the book of Matthew that quotes Jesus talking about this time that may come soon:

Matthew 10:28-39 ESV

²⁸And do not fear those who kill the body but cannot kill the soul. Rather fear Him who can destroy both soul and body in hell. ²⁹Are not two sparrows sold for a penny? And not one of them will fall to the ground apart from your Father. ³⁰But even the hairs of your head are all numbered. ³¹Fear not, therefore; you are of more value than many sparrows. ³²So everyone who acknowledges Me before men, I also will acknowledge before My Father who is in heaven, ³³but whoever denies Me before men, I also will deny before My Father who is in heaven. ³⁴Do not think that I have come to bring peace to the earth. I have not come to bring peace, but a sword. ³⁵For I have come to set a man against his father, and a daughter against her mother, and a daughter-in-law against her mother-in-law. ³⁶And a person's enemies will be those of his own household. ³⁷Whoever loves father or mother more than Me is not worthy of Me, and whoever loves son or daughter more than Me is not worthy of Me. ³⁸And whoever does not take his cross and follow Me is not worthy of Me. ³⁹Whoever finds his life will lose it, and whoever loses his life for My sake will find it.

Matthew 10:28-39 CEV
²⁸Don't be afraid of people. They can kill you, but they cannot harm your soul. Instead, you should fear God who can destroy both your body and your soul in hell. ²⁹Aren't two sparrows sold for only a penny? But your Father knows when any one of them falls to the ground. ³⁰Even the hairs on your head are counted. ³¹So don't be afraid! You are worth much more than many sparrows. ³²If you tell others that you belong to Me, I will tell my Father in heaven that you are My followers. ³³But if you reject Me, I will tell My Father in heaven that you don't belong to Me. ³⁴Don't think that I came to bring peace to the earth! I came to bring trouble, not peace. ³⁵I came to turn sons against their fathers, daughters against their mothers, and daughters-in-law against their mothers-in-law. ³⁶Your worst enemies will be in your own family. ³⁷If you love your father or mother or even your sons and daughters more than Me, you are not fit to be My disciples. ³⁸And unless you are willing to take up your cross and come with Me, you are not fit to be My disciples. ³⁹If you try to save your life, you will lose it. But if you give it up for Me, you will surely find it.

These are difficult and even frightening things to write and to read. But the Almighty Lord God is infinitely more powerful than Satan and his armies, and, since He is for us, who can be against us–and defeat us? We need to take heart and gather up our courage and remember what Romans 8 tells us:

Romans 8:31b-39 ESV
³¹If God is for us, who can be against us? ³²He who did not spare His own Son but gave Him up for us all, how will He not also with Him

graciously give us all things? ³³Who shall bring any charge against God's elect? It is God who justifies. ³⁴Who is to condemn? Christ Jesus is the one who died—more than that, who was raised— who is at the right hand of God, who indeed is interceding for us. ³⁵Who shall separate us from the love of Christ? Shall tribulation, or distress, or persecution, or famine, or nakedness, or danger, or sword? ³⁶As it is written, "For your sake we are being killed all the day long; we are regarded as sheep to be slaughtered." ³⁷No, in all these things we are more than conquerors through Him who loved us. ³⁸For I am sure that neither death nor life, nor angels nor rulers, nor things present nor things to come, nor powers, ³⁹nor height nor depth, nor anything else in all creation, will be able to separate us from the love of God in Christ Jesus our Lord.

Romans 8:31b-39 CEV

³¹If God is on our side, can anyone be against us? ³²God did not keep back His own Son, but He gave Him for us. If God did this, won't He freely give us everything else? ³³If God says His chosen ones are acceptable to Him, can anyone bring charges against them? ³⁴Or can anyone condemn them? No indeed! Christ died and was raised to life, and now He is at God's right side, speaking to Him for us. ³⁵Can anything separate us from the love of Christ? Can trouble, suffering, and hard times, or hunger and nakedness, or danger and death? ³⁶It is exactly as the Scriptures say, "For you we face death all day long. We are like sheep on their way to be butchered." ³⁷In everything we have won more than a victory because of Christ who loves us. ³⁸I am sure that nothing can separate us from God's love-not life or death, not angels or spirits, not the present or the future, ³⁹and not powers above or powers below. Nothing in all creation can separate us from God's love for us in Christ Jesus our Lord!

The signs of the times indicate that the time before the second coming of Jesus is growing short. You have only now to weigh the cost and make your decision, if you have not already done so. The evil in the world is mushrooming, and there will be intense pressure on you to conform your thinking and your living to the ways of the world. Just remember that Satan has been defeated but our Kinsman Redeemer has not yet thrown him out, so he still rules the world. Because Satan is a liar and the father of lies, the only language he and his followers speak is lying. They do not have your best interests at heart. Remember those things when you are enticed with what seems pleasant and pleasurable. Be sure your decisions line up with the Word of Jehovah, as it is given to us in the Bible.

For those who are adopted into the family of Jehovah, it will help us to keep a proper perspective if we can memorize the following verses that compare the suffering we will endure in this world with the unimaginable joys in the eternal life.

Romans 8:16-18 ESV

*^{16} The Spirit Himself bears witness with our spirit that we are children of God, ^{17}and if children, then heirs—heirs of God and fellow heirs with Christ, provided we suffer with Him in order that we may also be glorified with Him. ^{18}For I consider that **the sufferings of this present time are not worth comparing with the glory that is to be revealed to us.***

Romans 8:16-18 CEV

^{16}God's Spirit makes us sure that we are His children. ^{17}His Spirit lets us know that together with Christ we will be given what God has promised. We will also share in the glory of Christ, because we have suffered with Him. ^{18}I am sure that **what we are suffering now cannot compare with the glory that will be shown to us.**

2 Corinthians 4:16-18 ESV

*[16]So we do not lose heart. Though our outer nature is wasting away, our inner nature is being renewed day by day. [17]For **this slight momentary affliction is preparing for us an eternal weight of glory beyond all comparison,** [18]as we look not to the things that are seen but to the things that are unseen. For the things that are seen are transient, but **the things that are unseen are eternal.***

2 Corinthians 4:16-18 CEV

[16]We never give up. Our bodies are gradually dying, but we ourselves are being made stronger each day. [17]**These little troubles are getting us ready for an eternal glory that will make all our troubles seem like nothing**. [18]Things that are seen don't last forever, but **things that are not seen are eternal. That's why we keep our minds on the things that cannot be seen.**

PART THREE
In the World But Not of It

In John 15:19 (ESV), Jesus said to His followers, "If you were **of the world**, the world would love you as its own; but because you are **not of the world**, but I chose you out of the world, therefore the world hates you."

The passage in John 17:14-16 (ESV) also speaks of being "not of the world." In His prayer to His Father, Jesus said, "I have given them Your word, and the world has hated them because they are **not of the world**, just as I am **not of the world**. I do not ask that You take them out of the world, but that You keep them from the evil one. **They are not of the world, just as I am not of the world.**"

"The world" in the context of these two passages refers to the world system as it is currently governed by Satan and his fallen angels. "The world" is characterized by all the lies that Satan uses to deceive people and to blind them to the truth. "The world" is full of empty promises that cause people to seek after wealth, possessions, position, power over others, sex, fame, beauty, prestige, and the applause and approval of people. It is only when the desired goal has been actually attained that the person realizes it was all an illusion. It was all smoke and mirrors. It was all a lie. Sometimes it is not until the time of death that the person realizes his or her life was totally wasted. No one will remember them, and even if they do, what value will that be to the soul cast into outer darkness forever.

It is this world of lies in which we live. While there is much beauty in our earthly habitation, it is still governed by fallen people and fallen angels whose rebellious spirits make life miserable for themselves and everyone else. If we have been adopted into Jehovah's family, then our citizenship is no longer here in this world. It is in heaven.

Philippians 3:20-21 ESV

²⁰But **our citizenship is in heaven**, *and from it we await a Savior, the Lord Jesus Christ,* ²¹*Who will transform our lowly body to be like His glorious body, by the power that enables Him even to subject all things to Himself.*

Philippians 3:20-21 CEV

²⁰But **we are citizens of heaven** and are eagerly waiting for our Savior to come from there. Our Lord Jesus Christ ²¹has power over everything, and He will make these poor bodies of ours like His own glorious body.

This is how we live "in the world," but are not "of the world." We keep our eyes focused on working in the Family business of building His Kingdom until He returns. And, as travelers in a land not our own, we behave in such a way that brings honor to our Family name.

1 Peter 2:11-12 ESV

¹¹*Beloved, I urge you as sojourners and exiles to abstain from the passions of the flesh, which wage war against your soul.* ¹²*Keep your conduct among the Gentiles honorable, so that when they speak against you as evildoers, they may see your good deeds and glorify God on the day of visitation.*

1 Peter 2:11-12 CEV

¹¹Dear friends, you are foreigners and strangers on this earth. So I beg you not to surrender to those desires that fight against you. ¹²Always let others see you behaving properly, even though they may still accuse you of doing wrong. Then on the day of judgment, they will honor God by telling the good things they saw you do.

Jehovah Himself reached out to human beings and made it possible for us to have a relationship with Himself, after that relationship was lost at the time of the Fall of Adam and Eve. God the Son, Jesus Christ, became a human man, so that He could die in our place, to pay for our sins, and to remove our sins away from us permanently. Christianity is not a religion, with rules for people to follow so that Jehovah will accept them. It is a relationship, a family relationship that begins in this life, and goes on for eternity. This is a gift, a most precious gift, that is offered to all people, and should not be missed. Anyone who has claimed this free gift of life in the Family of God should naturally want those whom he knows and loves to be included as well. He should tell them what he has learned and has received, and extend the offer to them.

And when Jesus Christ has returned in glory, and has punished and removed all the evil people and evil spiritual beings from all creation, and has made the heavens and earth new, then the focus of the Family business will shift *from* building His Kingdom by bringing in new members of the Family, *to* ruling over the earth with Him. We will be allowed to fulfill the command that Adam failed to fulfill: to work with the Trinity (God the Father, God the Son, and God the Holy Spirit), in ruling over the earth.

There is an old document, written by men almost 400 years ago, which is called the Westminster Shorter Catechism. It says the "chief end of man is to glorify God and to enjoy Him forever." This means that the reasons people were created were to honor Jehovah and to enjoy being with Him forever! Jesus Christ's death and then His resurrection from the dead made it possible for us to be adopted into His family. Life in *that* family is what we were created for. To be and to live now and forever in *that* family is the purpose of this life. It is where we are loved fully. It is where we belong. It is where all our needs and wants are satisfied. It is our home.

Does God matter? YES, for now and for all eternity!

Jude 24-25 NASB

Now to Him who is able to keep you from stumbling, and to make you stand in the presence of His glory blameless with great joy, to the only God our Savior, through Jesus Christ our Lord, be glory, majesty, dominion and authority, before all time and now and forever. Amen.

Afterword

I am greatly indebted to the scholarly work of Dr. Michael S. Heiser for advancing my understanding of the Bible. The premise of his work is that the Bible must be studied from the viewpoint of the ancient Israelites and the first-century Jews. That is because their worldview, their context, was different from ours. They did not write or read with the Western filters of modern day Americans. The Biblical writers had their own worldview, and when we learn to read the Bible from that perspective, it opens up and expands our understanding of previously obscure passages.

The key difference from our Western approach to the Bible is that the writers of both the Old and New Testaments did not focus only or even primarily on this seen world which we inhabit. As Dr. Heiser says on page 15 of his book, *The Unseen Realm*, "[T]he intersection of our domain and the unseen world–which includes the triune God, but also a much more numerous cast–is at the heart of biblical theology."

As I wrote in the Preface, my goal in writing this book was to write, in plain English, an overview of the Bible's explanation of why the world is the way it is, and to share with readers the precious gift of eternal life through Jesus Christ that imparts meaning to my life.

I encourage every reader of this book, first and foremost, to prioritize and invest time reading and studying the Bible, praying for illumination and understanding from God the Holy Spirit as you read. As a secondary matter, I recommend the works of Dr. Heiser. His book, *The Unseen Realm*, is a highly academic book. It is well worth the time and effort it takes to get through it. He has made the same content available, however, in a condensed and easier-to-read book, *Supernatural*.

SDG

www.ingramcontent.com/pod-product-compliance
Lightning Source LLC
Chambersburg PA
CBHW050203130526
44591CB00034B/2065